A YEAR IN THE GARDEN

with Stuart Jackson

at heart ♡ publications   ★ The Star

First published in 2006 by:
First Edition Limited, 32 Stamford Street,
Altrincham, Cheshire, WA14 1EY

in conjunction with
The Star, York Street, Sheffield, S1 1PU

ISBN: 1-84547-105-9

Contents

INTRODUCTION

After spending a lifetime in gardening, both as a passionate amateur grower/exhibitor and also earning my living from the industry, I can say without hesitation that gardening is by no means an exact science. It never has been and never will be with all the uncertainties of weather, pests, disease and the like. So why do we do it, and is it worthwhile?

Of course it is, for gardening is all about sharing friendships and experiences and, well, sheer satisfaction and enjoyment. I often remark that if gardening was easy and everything went strictly to order and as planned, it would lose its attraction and become mundane and boring. Nothing beats the thrill of seeing a tiny dust-like seed germinate and grow into a joyous thing of beauty.

Whether we grow flowers for their wonderful colour and beauty, fruit and vegetables for their exquisite and unbeatable home-grown taste, or spend our time chasing the 'red cards' at shows, the world of gardening is so diverse and the possibilities endless.

Over my many years in gardening, starting with my first garden – an allotment at number 108 Morley Street, Sheffield, in the early fifties (yes, I was born very young at an early age!) – gardening has been my passion. The changes I've seen in that time, both commercially and for the amateur gardener, have been enormous. Yes, the winds of change are not blowing but rather howling a gale. Hybrids, composts, hydroponics, recycling, systemic and foliar feeding, to name but a few, have all either evolved or been completely revamped in my lifetime.

I well remember in the fifties riding to my allotment through snow in May on my old Ariel motorbike with a gallon of paraffin in a pannier on the back. The sole purpose was to fill my greenhouse heater as tomato plants had been planted the week previous. Such dedication!

Today, of course, with thermostatically controlled electric fan heaters, it's another ball game altogether.

Whether you have a tiny paved area, a sunny balcony, or a very large garden, it matters not; the most important thing is that it is yours and, thanks to modern science and technology, the world truly is your oyster. Gardening is a fun subject, so let's have fun! Gardening is very much a personal matter but there really is something for everyone.

Traditions die hard and so many of the myths, legends and folklore of yesteryear have an element of truth in them based on sound common sense and practice. Soot, sulphur, vinegar, sheep droppings, wool shoddy and bicarbonate of soda all have a part to play in that vast galaxy of know-how from the past and, coupled with today's scientists, they ensure gardening will go from strength to strength.

In my formative years, I set out as a technical 'rep', bright-eyed and bushy-tailed, to put the commercial growers' world to rights. In those days, nurseries were vast, sprawling areas of Dutch light-type greenhouses with lots of people hard at work with soil heaps, steam boilers, potting sheds, barrows and turf stacks. Today, of course, it is so different; they are not so much nurseries as plant factories. Compost delivered in bulk by tipper wagons, conveyor belts, pot-

filling machinery, seeders that drop one tiny seed into each small cell segment, automatic watering, feeding, spraying, shading, heating... the whole system computer-controlled at the flick of a switch. Such is progress!

This country's nurserymen, scientists and plant breeders are very much leaders in their fields, so our gardening future, I'm certain, is assured, so worry not.

May I quote an old Chinese proverb –

"If you would be happy for a week,
Take a wife.
If you would be happy for a month,
Kill a pig.
But if you would be happy all of your life,
Plant a garden."

(With apologies to she who must be obeyed!)

Happy gardening!

JOBS FOR JANUARY

Your top priority is to wash and sterilise pots and trays ready for sowing in your greenhouse. Put a bag of compost in your greenhouse to warm.

BROAD BEANS: Sow, even in a cold greenhouse, singly in three inch pots. I prefer square type.

ONION SETS: Set in trays of seed compost leaving just the tips exposed. Cover with fleece if frost threatens. Heat-treated sets are worth the extra cost as they do not bolt and give a heavier yield.

FRUIT: For summer fruiting raspberries, tip just an inch from each cane to promote stronger fruiting laterals.

PONDS: If you have a pond, float a rubber ball in it to ensure at least part is kept ice-free.

SOIL TESTS: Use a D.I.Y kit (available from your local garden centre) or send off to a specialist laboratory.

JANUARY

Non-gardeners always ask what we dedicated plant-lovers find to do in January, but it is an extremely busy month, irrespective of the weather.

Start the New Year with a gardening diary. Nothing elaborate, just a simple notebook to suit you and your garden. I suggest you list such things as weather, temperatures, seed and plant purchases and sources, planting dates, crop details, and past results and comments for future reference. Examples of notes on some of my past results include, "v. v. good" down to the simple instruction' "drop" – perhaps you could use the letters "N.B.G" in lieu of "drop"!

Clean up is very much a must for January. Pots, trays, canes, the greenhouse and coldframes should all be washed and sterilised for the coming season. Ensure greenhouse glass is really clean to compensate for the poor winter light. You should also use this time to oil, clean and sharpen all your garden tools.

January – subject to weather – is a great month for maintenance like painting fences, post and outdoor structures. Winter digging should have been completed prior to Christmas, but if not, now is the time to do it. Black polythene sheets or cloches can be placed over soil to warm it for the earliest vegetable crops.

Spring bulbs, daffodils, crocuses and early tulips should all be removed from coldframes and brought into the greenhouse. As flower shoots begin to emerge and colour starts to appear, transfer them into your home to brighten up the winter gloom.

Weather warning – if snow settles on trees and shrubs, knock it off gently as branches can so easily break under the weight of the snow. I use a stout six-foot garden cane.

Leave snow on garden frames as it acts as an insulator, but if snow settles on your greenhouse roof, introduce a gentle heat source into the greenhouse. The old tip of a lighted candle or night-lite placed under a large inverted clay plant pot works a treat.

Yes, it's all go in January!

Happy New Year. Yes, here we go again on the great gardening carousel with a clean canvas but lots of hope and aspirations. I am delighted to firmly state that our plantsmen have really done us proud with a plethora of new species and varieties to both inspire and, perhaps, challenge us.

Specimen or dot plants are always highly prized as they are so architecturally pleasing and give our beds height, contrast and, of course, focal points. Dare I say the Victorian formal gardens used this type of plant to telling effect and they are again very much in vogue. Yes, it all goes full circle!

On my tours and visits last summer, these plants were very much in evidence and so I've selected three newcomers for your approval and approbation - all will certainly be grown by yours truly. All are available as seed and should be grown as half-hardy annuals.

Let me start by acquainting you with the startling Ornamental Millet - Pennisetum Purple Majesty. This grows to four or five feet high with purple plumes at least a foot long. Backed by deep purple stems and foliage it will certainly make a great focal point in summer flowerbeds. It requires full sun to attain a deep purple hue. Seed is not cheap but the effect is truly spectacular.

Another member of the herb family - basil – is my second newcomer. This is Ornamental Basil - Oriental Breeze, which is a dwarfer, standing at approximately two and a half feet with dark green foliage and dark red flowers. A dual-purpose plant as you can snip off a leaf or two and use for culinary purposes, whilst also enjoying its fragrance and beauty. A low-priced seed but a great performer and well worth a place in your beds and borders.

Specimen plants are highly prized: they're so architecturally pleasing

Love Lies Bleeding (the Amaranthus) is well known to cottage gardeners, seemingly dating back forever in gardening folklore and very highly regarded. My last selection is a member of this family but, instead of trailing, it stands proudly upright and needing no support, making it an ideal dot plant. Depending on which catalogue you study, the foliage colour is defined as velvety mauve, purple or red. All agree, however, that the flower plumes are red. As ever, a good sunny position will help to intensify the colour plus an occasional dose of high potash liquid feed.

So there are three totally different plants to consider all with form, shape and intense colour - I commend them to you.

GARDEN TIPS

- Unless frozen, now is the time to prune honeysuckle (Lonicera). Cut back at least one-third and if there are many shoots, prune the oldest to ground level. Feed and mulch after pruning.

- Hellebores - both Niger and Orientalis - are now coming into bloom. Carefully cut off any leaves badly marked with black spot fungal disease, a regular problem with these plants.

Dual-purpose: Ornamental basil is not only a beautiful plant but can be used for culinary purposes, too

Here we are, January and a whole new gardening year - aren't we lucky? Please forgive me for being rather smug and perhaps a trifle immodest, but the news from the UK seed industry that veg sales have, for the first time, exceeded flower seed sales, is joy to my ears. Whether it's the move to healthier living and organic growing, I know not, but nothing can compare with well-grown home fruit and veg. Allotments are now the in-thing, with many councils having lengthy waiting lists. I certainly recall my allotment years with great affection.

So, to the present...let's start with the king spud, perhaps today's star. Potatoes are so adaptable and so easy to grow. Forget the yield on extra early types, it's the challenge and, above all, the taste that inspires.

Spuds come in many shapes and colours, but also in groups, i.e. extra early, first early, second early and main crop. Let us concentrate on the first two, which can be grown in outdoor beds (under fleece), in pots, containers or grow bags in either a cold greenhouse or a deep frame.

Start by obtaining 'certified' seed potatoes that are specialist raised. The earliest types are available now so order promptly. On receipt, these need setting up to 'chit', i.e. produce growing shoots from the dormant eyes. Place them, rose-end up (I find egg boxes ideal for this) and place in good light on a sunny window sill or greenhouse shelf.

A good tip is to add a drop or two of high nitrogen liquid feed to lukewarm water and spray lightly over to promote strong shoots. When the shoots are an inch or so long they are ready for planting. Special potato planting barrels are widely available and can be used under glass or on a sheltered patio. However, I simply cut a grow bag in two lengthways, then stand each half upright to make two polybags, then place in a cold greenhouse.

In pots and containers, crock well and use a rich growing medium and only just cover the tubers leaving lots of room for topping up. As the foliage emerges keep adding a little more compost till the pot is full. On really cold nights, drape horticultural fleece over the top and fasten plastic bubble wrap around the container to deter frost. As growth increases give doses of liquid feed.

As a guide, I plant two tubers in a 12-inch pot, three in a 15-inch and six in a growbag, three in each half. May sound a lot of trouble, but to taste real new potatoes at Easter is priceless.

Selected varieties suggested:
EXTRA-EARLY - Lady Christi, Accent, Rocket and Swift
FIRST EARLY - Winston, Maris Bard
SECOND EARLY - Maris Peer (for the real Boston new potato taste)
SALAD POTATOES - Ratte, Pink Fir Apple

GARDEN TIPS

- Set up seed potatoes to chit. I place mine on a high shelf in the greenhouse for maximum light. Also, have horticultural fleece to hand to cover on frosty nights. Remove fleece each morning.

- Chrysanthemum growers, it's high time to start taking cuttings. Use bottom heat and dip base of cuttings in rooting hormone powder or gel.

Potatoes are so adaptable and so easy to grow

Extra early: Stuart shows off his own crop of potatoes

Probably the biggest phenomenon in gardening in the last decade has been the fantastic sales of plug plants. Starting as something of a novelty, they have now reached incredible proportions, and rightly so, as they have brought plant-raising of the more difficult varieties down to a simple procedure.

The UK industry has been very much at the forefront of the development of plugs; mini-plants, seedlings and garden-ready plants (both seed and cutting raised) are available in an ever-increasing range.

For readers with a greenhouse equipped with a little heating, small plugs and seedlings are a good buy in March.

Over the past year or so, the range of both salad and veg plants in plug format has greatly increased to cope with the upsurge in their popularity. Whilst not every variety is covered, the most popular sellers are on offer widely. Special praise is due, I feel, to the quality of the packaging and how this new segment of our industry is really being nurtured and streamlined with the home gardeners in mind.

As ever, you get what you pay for and seedling/plug sizes vary from company to company.

For readers with a greenhouse equipped with a little heating, small plugs and seedlings are a good buy in March. Readers with only a coldframe or cold greenhouse should look for larger plugs and defer delivery until April. In all cases, have horticultural fleece to hand for use in a sudden cold spell.

Handy: A tray of plug plants all ready for potting

Plugs represent a great way to both plan and fill your garden and for fundraisers with a little time and greenhouse facilities to spare, a novel opportunity to help your cause.

Here's a quiz question for you: What do bulbs, corms, tubers and rhizomes have in common? Answer: They are all the swollen stems/leaves/roots of plants that contain the embryo of the next generation of blooms - your garden's sleeping beauties.

As I'm so fond of saying, when you buy a bag of bulbs you are actually buying a bag of flowers. All that's needed is light, warmth and moisture to give a riot of pleasure and colour.

I never cease to marvel in the grey winter months at the sight of snowdrops, aconites and crocuses, emerging in all their glory to be followed, in succession, with anemone blanda, iris reticulata and danfordiae, narcissi, daffodils, cyclamen coum, tulips...the list goes on and on.

These plant factories, or storehouses, are so trouble-free for both expert and novice gardeners alike. They are of special interest to the new gardener and a great introduction to gardening for children - a real hands-on experience.

A word of advice: with the exception of rhizomes and, in particular, flag and bearded iris, many amateurs do not plant deep enough. Ideally, all will benefit from good drainage and on heavy soil apply grit or horticultural sand liberally.

What is the difference between the four types, you ask? Well, simply, bulbs are swollen leaves that produce, below ground level, a smooth fleshy mass with the embryo flower already formed in the base, e.g. daffodils and garlic.

Good examples of corms are crocuses and gladioli. These form each year on top of the old one, just needing careful lifting, drying and cleaning at the end of their growing cycle.

Examples of tubers, which are actually swollen roots, are dahlias, cyclamen and, of course, that staple vegetable, the potato. The old tubers die after flowering, hence the reason for

GARDEN TIPS

- The universal aid to storing bulbs, corms, tubers and rhizomes and to deter storage rot or mildew is to dust with sulphur powder. Store dry, cool, but frost-free. Use trays or paper bags, not polythene.

- For good snowdrops, always buy and plant these 'in the green'; that is, young plants after flowering, not dried bulbs. They will be available from February onwards. Look out for them. A sure way to success.

Blooming great: A riot of spring flowers - March in my garden gives me great pleasure

not lifting tubers until all growth is finished and the new tubers are fully formed.

Finally, rhizomes are swollen, underground stems often growing as gnarled, hard, horizontal clumps on the soil surface, bearded iris being a perfect example. Do remember, that in common they all have the stored energy to give great joy, but help them along with a little TLC by giving moisture, good drainage and occasional feeding.

Their world is a wonder of nature - cherish them.

JOBS FOR FEBRUARY

LAWNS: This is the month I send my mower to be serviced ready for the hard season ahead.

CLEMATIS: Prune all large, late flowering types hard back; also passion flowers.

FRUIT: Gooseberries are now coming into leaf. Dress the root area with sulphate of potash - 2oz per sq yard.

VEGETABLE PATCH: Subject to weather, mark out the various beds. Manure or lime depending on crop to be grown. Cover ground with black plastic sheeting to both dry and warm for the earliest crops.

GREENHOUSE: In a heated propagator (20°C), sow F1 hybrid geranium seeds as they require a long season. Take chrysanthemum cuttings, both early and late varieties. Sow sweet pea seeds in sweet pea tubes or use the cardboard core from toilet rolls.

FEBRUARY

Usually cold and dreary, February signals mid winter. Beat the blues by bringing into your home potted spring bulbs to lift your spirits. There's lots to do in the greenhouse, like taking chrysant cuttings, picking the first early potatoes and starting your broad beans and onion sets. Make sure you ventilate the greenhouse on warmer days.

Outdoors, late February is an ideal time to prune late flowering clematis, passion flowers and honeysuckles. Note however, that it is still too early north of the River Trent to prune roses.

It's also time to start thinking about your lawn. If the weather permits, scarify/spike your lawn to improve drainage. Another good tip is to sow grass seed in a standard seed tray on just 1 inch of level compost. Place it in the greenhouse and keep frost-free. This makes an ideal patch for repairing bare spots in your lawn in early March or April. Always have a patch ready – it's good insurance for lawn problems.

Towards the end of the month, you should start to prepare your sweet pea trenches ready for late March planting.

For gardeners – and greenhouse owners, in particular –
February is certainly an exciting and challenging time.

I assume all readers have by now sent off their orders for seeds, seedlings and plug plants for the coming season and eagerly await delivery. We certainly have so much going for us these days but I feel a few reminders are called for.

Onion sets – such a favourite – but may I remind readers that, apart from the many varieties available, certain suppliers also offer heat-treated onion sets. These, as the name implies, have had this additional treatment which both increases the yield and deters bolting. Well worth the extra, I suggest.

I strongly urge you to invest in a tin of Cheshunt Compound, a time-honoured ancient cure that has really stood the test of time

Dare I mention potatoes again? Well, now available from certain specialist growers are pre-chitted tubers. This means that on delivery they are already in active growth and ready for planting; again, a real plus point.

One regular problem with seed sowing, and one that can also occur with plug plants, is the dreaded 'damping-off' disease. Here, I strongly urge you to invest in a tin of Cheshunt Compound, a time-honoured ancient cure that has really stood the test of time. I use this on all my seed sowing/cutting composts, irrespective of variety. I find one tin lasts me two seasons so is excellent value and, more importantly, I enjoy a high success ratio with my plant production.

Liquid feeding is high on my attention to detail activities and I use a range of various NPK formulations. Weak, and I stress weak, doses of high nitrogen, applied at room temperature or slightly above, does wonders to jolt into life dormant, over-wintered begonia tubers, chrysanthemum stools (to promote basal cuttings), fuschias and dahlia tubers. I also use it on my seed potato tubers to encourage shoots.

A very specialised formulation, rare, but well worth seeking out is a 1-4-1 ratio used by commercial growers. This is, of course, extremely high in phosphates, the root forming

GARDEN TIPS

- Vegetable growers should mark out, and cover with black polythene, beds for onion sets/broad beans that have been started in a greenhouse or coldframe. They will warm up and dry for March planting.

- Sow antirrhinums (snap dragons) in gentle heat (15-18°C) now. They need a long season of growth to give off their best. Some great new varieties.

Know your onions: Attention to detail produces a perfect, prize-winning matched set of onions

NATIONAL
VEGETABLE
SOCIETY

agent. I use this, again at a very weak ratio, on seedlings and cuttings. I apply this only from January to April but it really does promote the plant's healthy roots in abundance.

Finally, may I remind readers that bicarbonate of soda is back on the approved list of products for use by amateur gardeners? This is a very old folklore remedy for fungal plant diseases, in particular, mildew on grape vines. Spray at 1oz per quart of water in February before growth begins.

Yes, by using the old and the new we really have it all going for us – long may it continue.

Prizewinners: Mel Ednie and his wife show off their giant 15lb 11 3/4 oz onion at Harrogate

TAKING THE CHALLENGE

Chairing a recent gardeners' question time promotes
this week's offering as a change from the norm.

One rather unusual question promoted quite a stir from all involved, namely, why are some so-called 'easy plants' so darned hard to grow for so many? The plant in question was Meconopsis, that gorgeous blue hardy Himalyan poppy that, once established, self-seeds like crazy.

My personal thoughts immediately went back many years to my mother's incredible success with lily of the valley (Convallaria Majalis), another plant that so many find problems in getting established. This bed of spring delight received scant attention (sorry mum), but each spring the multitude of bright shiny pips of new growth emerged without fail to be followed with sheaths of green mini tulip-like foliage and nodding stems of fragrant white bells. Many side clumps were dug up and given to friends, late April being the ideal time.

With regard to Meconopsis you need to have humus-rich, well drained, semi-shaded soil and use well rotted farmyard manure (FYM)/garden compost. Go easy on chemical fertilisers, and grow from selected named seed varieties or buy-in young plants from a specialist source. Patience is obviously needed and they can be difficult, but are so rewarding and once established, no problem.

Parsley, that traditional herb, is often another problem child. The old folklore tip of pouring a kettleful of boiling water over it after you have prepared your seed bed and prior to sowing often does the trick...try it.

Another plant that can present problems is wisteria. In my book, a climber/wall cover par excellence. Yes, it does take years to clothe a wall, and yes, it's not the cheapest of plants, but so worth the effort. My specimen is over 80-feet long, trained horizontally and a real April/May treat.

Always buy a grafted plant, look for the graft bump as in roses, prepare the site extra well and keep well watered. There are two well-known forms in shades of white, blue and mauve: Sinensis and Hortensis, and both are great.

And here's another quiz question for you: how do you tell the difference? Answer: one twines clockwise the other anti-clockwise. Not a lot of people know this!

GARDEN TIPS

- F1 hybrid geranium: Sow seed now if you can give bottom heat - 20/22 °C is ideal. It'll need a long season of growth but is a great bedder. After germination, give it maximum light and reduce temperature to approximately 15°C.

- Broad beans: Only need a coldframe or greenhouse. Sow singly in three-inch pots, large cell trays or root trainers. Will produce super plants for March planting and they are good for you!

Sound advice: You should always buy a grafted wisteria plant

TIME TO GET TOUGH ON YOUR TREES AND SHRUBS

*P*runing – a word that fills many with trepidation! Basically, we prune to keep trees and bushes in shape, to promote flowers, fruit and berries and, most essentially, to remove dead or diseased material.

In a nutshell, it is far better to be brave and prune hard than to snip off bits here and there.

In a nutshell, it is far better to be brave and prune hard than to snip off bits here and there. Always prune in steps, stand back and view from all sides (remember, you can't glue branches back), use clean, sharp tools and have courage.

Fruit trees need immediate attention, all except plums, which we summer prune in July/August.

There are two schools of thought regarding sealing wounds after removing thicker branches, say two inches in diameter.

I personally suggest you do use a sealant to deter the ingress of fungal diseases. The old allotment trick of using any lead-based paint has always worked for me.

Clematis always promote pruning queries. Actually, all you need to know to ensure success is the variety name. Basically, they fall into three groups so always retain the label. From then on it's child's play.

Group three covers the large flowering mid-summer types, so very popular, and now is pruning time. Be bold, cut them hard back to just above a green leaf bud, feed and mulch – job's done.

Leave rose bush pruning till mid to late March in the Sheffield area.

Always prune in steps, stand back and view from all sides (remember, you can't glue branches back), use clean, sharp tools and have courage.

GARDEN TIPS

- Plant Jerusalem artichokes under cloches. (Note: they are not from Jerusalem but America and a member of the sunflower family!)

- Give rhubarb a light dressing of sulphate of ammonia to speed up growth.

Tough love: Dogwood must be pruned back to ground level

TAKE IT AS RED FOR A TASTY TOMATO CROP!

What is by far the favourite amateur greenhouse summer crop? Yes, you've guessed it: tomatoes.

Now is the time to make plans for these. For a bumper crop, if there's a little heat available, a start can be made any time now.

A steady growth pattern and maximum light is needed to give sturdy, short-jointed plants for April planting. Growbags or large pots (12 inches minimum diameter) are ideal for the final potting, and always ensure containers, canes and greenhouse are scrupulously clean.

Use fresh, sterile compost. My choice, dare I say, is a peat-based variety, plus ten per cent John Innes No. 3 to give a little bulk.

F1 hybrid varieties have certainly come up trumps with a welter of new varieties released each season to tempt us. My advice to new greenhouse owners is to grow two or three varieties and have a family taste test.

Regular attention to watering, side-shooting and supporting, plus a continuous feeding regime should, hopefully, give great results.

I personally grow just five or, at the most, six trusses per plant and use a cold electric fan to both cool and give fresh air circulation during hot spells. And yes, it's worth all the effort - the taste is superb.

GARDEN TIPS

- Fill in your sweet pea trenches now and erect the canes ready for late March planting. Finish off the beds with a dusting of lime.

- A first sowing of early type stumpy carrots can be made now, either in a coldframe (six inch depth of fine soil) or 10 inches diameter pots in a cold greenhouse. Ready end of April.

Colourful newcomer: Hybrid tomato Sparta

Stuart tends to his beloved tomato plants

JOBS FOR MARCH

SWEET PEAS: Plant out towards the end of the month. Plant firmly and tie to supporting canes.

VEGETABLE PATCH: Sow your first row of early garden peas and first early potatoes. Cover with horticultural fleece or cloches for a flying start.

PRUNING: ROSES, late flowering clematis and passion flowers should all be pruned this month.

GREENHOUSE: Sow half hardy annual flower seeds, use gentle bottom heat. Continue to take chrysant cuttings. Set up to sprout dormant dahlia tubers, tuberous begonias and gloxinas. Take tip cuttings of fuschias.

COLDFRAMES: A great asset. Use them for hardening off rooted chrysant cuttings, onions, leeks and onion sets ready for April plantings.

LAWNS: If dry enough make first cut - don't scalp!

MARCH

March is a really hectic month for gardeners, especially where the greenhouse is concerned.

It's time to sow your choice of half hardy annuals. Take a tip from me: gentle bottom heat is invaluable. You should also use really clean seed trays and pots, and sow thinly. I use cheshunt compound against the dreaded damping-off disease, Botrytis.

Start growing your begonia and gloxinia tubers. Plant them hollow-side up in trays or pots, and just set them level in compost. Pot-up dormant dahlia tubers – again, gentle bottom heat will help.

Take more chrysant and fuschia cuttings and transfer them to a coldframe. Now is also a good time to sow tomato and cucumber seeds, and to make the first sowings (under cloches or in a coldframe) of carrots (use stump-rooted), lettuce, radishes and spring onions for early salads.

Outdoors – yes, it's rose pruning month! It's also time to cut the grass for the first time this year. Be careful not to scalp it; and bear in mind that it's too early to feed or treat.

Towards the end of the month, plant out sweet pea plants. Also, "pre-chitted" first, early potatoes (under fleece) and onion sets.

Lastly, if you can, do take time out to visit early spring shows. You'll be amazed at the latest plants and ideas.

As Easter - a major landmark in both the Christian and gardener's calendar - is almost upon us, what better plant to share with you than that exotic climber, the Passion Flower, the most popular variety being the hardy Passiflora Caerulea?

On countless occasions I've been asked about this plant, not so much about the pruning and cultivation, but the fruit, which is often produced in late summer/early autumn. These invariably follow a hot summer the previous year, which induces fruit production. Are these edible, you ask? Well to quote my old mum, "The taste's nowt to write home about!" Yes, they are related to the passion fruit sold as a delicacy and are edible, but frankly, not for me.

Passion flowers are great climbers for growing on a pergola, fence or arbor; all they ask is good light, sun and plenty of moisture; in other words, a little TLC. They do best in a south, west or southwest facing position. They are quite rampant growers once established, so allow them room to expand. A good thick organic mulch does wonders and feeding with a high potash fertiliser stimulates flower and, dare I say, fruit production.

Once established, pruning passion flowers is a simple operation. Wait until March when new growth becomes quite evident then prune down to 12-18 inches just above a plump leaf bud. They can be container grown quite successfully, all you need to use is a large container - a half barrel is ideal - plus adequate drainage holes and well crocked. John Innes No. 3 compost is the best growing medium in my opinion.

Whilst, as mentioned, Passiflora Caerulea is the most popular and widely grown variety, a whole family awaits your exploration. Some are relatively tender so a greenhouse or conservatory is needed, or at the very least, position in a sheltered south-facing spot.

There are many variants on the Christian legend of the passion flower, but I feel the best is the one handed down from the Spanish missionaries who first discovered the plant in Brazil in the 17th century. This goes: "The outer corona represents the countless disciples; the ten sepals and petals of the bloom, the ten true apostles - leave out Peter who denied Christ three times and Judas; the fringed corolla, the crown of thorns; the five stamens, the five mounds of Christ; the ovary, the sponge dipped in vinegar; the three styles, the three nails used to crucify him; and the central stem they grow from, the true stem of the cross."

Happy gardening and Happy Easter.

P.S. Whilst garden centres do a yeoman job, should you wish to explore a fuller range of these exotic cultivars, contact The National Collection of Passiflora, Lampley Road, Kingston Seymour, Clevedon, North Somerset, BS21 6XS who offer both plants and seeds by mail order.

GARDEN TIPS

- Have you had your lawn mower serviced for the coming season?

- Now is the time to sow half-hardy annual (HHA) bedders, in gentle bottom heat, in a greenhouse. Sow thinly and use cheshunt compound against the dreaded damping off disease.

The passion flower: Enjoy its beauty but not its fruit!

PERFECT TIME TO ENSURE YOU GET BEAUTIFUL ROSES

I have lost track of the number of times I've stressed the dangers of pruning roses too early.

This is based on many years' experience, and the recent very cold spell certainly proved my point. To prune too early and then to be followed by a really cold spell can cause disaster with fresh, tender growth suffering from dieback.

However, gardening is not an exact science and plants are very resilient. But now, or over the next two weeks, is ideal rose pruning time.

The golden pruning rules still apply, namely, the weaker the growth, the harder we prune. This sounds an anomaly but does promote sturdier growth. Strong growers prune less hard.

Wherever possible, prune to just above an outward facing leaf bud - this makes for the open, goblet-shaped form we desire. Start by cutting back to ground level all dead wood and any crossing branches. Remember, we aim for an open structure.

It goes without saying that really sharp secateurs make for good, clean cuts and you should carefully remove all debris - a great source of spreading mildew and blackspot.

Speaking of diseases, I have no hesitation in recommending Roseclear 3, though not for organic gardeners. This is a chemical-based combined insecticide/fungicide designed to control aphids of all shades and blackspot and mildew diseases, the prime problems that beset roses. Use this on a monthly basis starting after pruning is completed.

Finally, give a dressing of rose fertiliser topped with a good organic mulch at least two inches deep – three inches is even better.

The choice can be quite bewildering when one considers the vast number of new additions released annually, with so many launched at Chelsea each May.

However, I firmly believe roses should have good perfume so do the smell test or check the specialist rose catalogues. For ground cover, Flower Carpet still reigns supreme in my book and is very healthy.

Enjoy your roses!

ROSE TIPS

- Epsom salts (magnesium sulphate) is a great tonic for roses. It really does give the plants a glossy foliage and good health. Give your beds a sprinkling round each bush in April and again in June. Don't forget to water in well.

- Deadheading roses is very important if they are to maintain their flowering. Cut faded blooms back at least six inches to encourage further flowers. Burn prunings.

Full bloom: Wisley, bred by David Austin Roses and named after the RHS show garden

Our first essential this spring should be to replace in our soil the vital nutrients that have leached away. Good old FYM/garden compost will do wonders, but it's really a case of digging deeper into our pockets and applying more fertilisers.

The plus point is that competition is fierce, so good bargains are available and bulk buying by sharing with friends or neighbours is strongly suggested. I realise the choice can be bewildering, but I recommend the natural, bulkier, organic types. My mind immediately turns to the concentrated pelleted types, such as chicken, horse, cow, seaweed, spent hops, etc. My reasoning is that they will, apart from being quite slow acting, actually help to build up both the humus content and the soil structure.

Containers are a great way of presenting a bright early start to herald summer.

Containers are a great way of presenting a bright early start to herald summer. Plug plants just get bigger and better and, in so many cases, cheaper - a spin-off from improved cultural methods.

The wide range of containers never ceases to amaze me. A few years ago, stainless steel and stark, straight forms were all the rage. Now a complete change for softer, woven basket forms holds sway. Whatever you choose, the world truly is your oyster.

I like the concept of a 'movable' display, starting with containers mounted on small castors so that you can alter your vista instantly.

The old wooden wheelbarrow is an old tried and tested feature, but a garden down at

Sutton Bridge, Lincolnshire, always takes my eye. This is a tiny front cottage garden that has an old Swallow brand boat-shaped child's pram, hood down, totally filled with pots of colourful 'bedders' - beat that!

GARDEN TIPS

● As a golden rule, always add slow release fertiliser granules and water retaining granules to your container compost - great time savers that make for a super display.

● Save coffee jar lids, they make great 'feet' for your containers/window boxes to ensure air circulation underneath...and they're free!

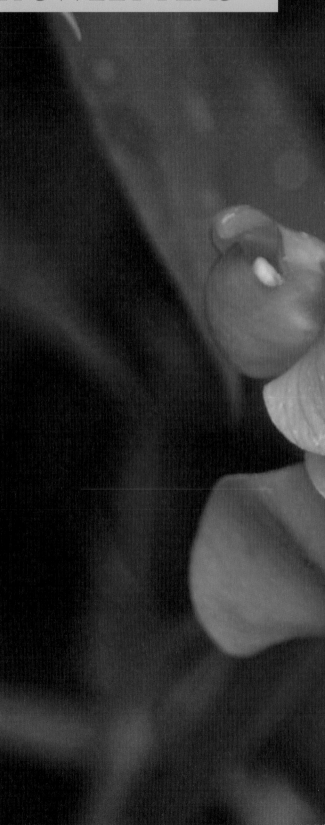

For sheer beauty, perfume and dainty charm, sweet peas take some beating. They are much tougher than their fragile appearance portrays, for once established they grow and produce blooms at quite a fantastic rate of knots.

For home gardeners, do consider sweet peas; they'll amply repay your efforts. For serious growing they are best grown in a double row of 8ft canes on the single cordon system. Give good light, keep well tied and, above all, cut blooms regularly - don't let them set seed or flowering will cease.

A simple method to grow them is in a circular wigwam of 8ft canes, tied at the top set and at the back of flower beds to give height and character.

Sweet pea seeds are quite cheap to buy, or you can buy in young plants in March/April from several specialist sources. They love planting in a deep, well drained, sunny spot and are quite thirsty plants.

Do take note that if raising your own plants they need stopping after two pairs of leaves have formed, as the next shoot produced is far stronger. Plant out from the end of March onwards, stand back and enjoy them - they truly are a treasure.

Sweet Peas:
Their charm and beauty are hard to beat

SWEET PEA TIPS

- A long tap root is the hallmark of sweet peas so sow the seed in long sweet pea tubes or use the cardboard tube from toilet rolls - they're ideal.

- Being a member of the Legume family, go easy on the nitrogenous fertilisers. Aim for lots of phosphates and potash - they are the key to show-winning blooms.

JOBS FOR APRIL

Always a busy month for sowing/planting.

FLOWER BEDS: Dead-head daffs as they finish, and give a liquid boost of high potash liquid fertiliser or dust the area with sulphate of potash to plump up the bulbs for next season. Plant gladioli corms; bed on grit sand if soil is heavy/wet.

VEGETABLE PATCH: Sow pumpkins, cucumbers, melons, courgettes and runner beans singly in three-inch pots for planting out in May.

GREENHOUSE: Harden off plug/bedding plants ready for May planting. Fill hanging baskets but have these in your greenhouse to develop - hang outside in May.

LAWNS: Now is the time for applying selective weed killer/weed 'n' feed/summer lawn feed depending on the condition of your lawn. Cut and edge lawns every week.

APRIL

Another hectic month for gardeners and, particularly in the North, one that can be fraught with danger due to late frosts. April is certainly a month for transferring plants to garden frames and cloches for hardening off.

This is a very important month for lawn maintenance in preparation for a long summer ahead (fingers crossed, anyway!). Time to apply fertiliser and/or selective lawn weed killer and moss control. It's also a great month for laying new lawns, whether using turf or seed.

It's a little too early for planting cold house tomatoes, cucumbers and peppers, and certainly too cold for outdoor tomatoes...wait until next month. Do, however, use the time to look out for bargains and special offers on composts and plug plants.

Take my tip...if you own a greenhouse, make up your hanging baskets this month and hang them inside it. They will be superb next month for hanging outside for instant appeal.

As an alternative, do consider a basket of mint or mixed herbs hung by the kitchen door – it's ideal for the head of cooking without getting wet feet! Or plant tomatoes or strawberries in baskets – they make colourful and rewarding alternatives, and remember... slugs can't fly!

Make sure compost, slow-release fertiliser and water-retaining granules are bought-in for the big container, patio planter, window-box filling time of early May.

It's also time to start work on the vegetable patch. Plant most veg in the open ground this month, except runner beans, sweetcorn, cucumbers and pumpkins, which are all frost-tender so delay a few weeks until the weather picks up.

P.S. Slugs, snails and vine weevil are all very active this month so take necessary precautions. I buy-in nematodes and natural predators for use in early May – remember, they need to be kept in a fridge which is quite safe, I promise you, as the packaging is always first class.

CHALLENGE OF THE NEW

Help! Can anyone offer me a rubber-sided greenhouse? As usual at this time of year, mine is really full, not to mention the five large frames, cloches and large plastic domes also adorning my garden!

This is the most exciting, but perhaps also the most stressful time of year, mainly spent keeping all the young plants progressing well. The key is, don't overproduce; it is easy to go overboard and no one wants to commit mass horticultural infanticide!

Regular readers know that every year I grow 70-80 per cent of tried and tested flowers and veg and the remainder are new varieties that I saw last year on many visits to trial grounds. These I saw grown to perfection so they really set my pulses racing. Our hobby is certainly vast - I'm reliably informed that amateur gardeners are the ninth largest contributor to the country's economy - a princely sum.

As in so many walks of life, many newcomers flit briefly across the horizon and then sink into obscurity. However, hope springs eternal and we all look for another cracker.

In the last decade or so, Surfinia Petunias, Fiesta, the double Busy Lizzie, Dichondra Silver Falls (by far my number one hanging basket foliage plant), Tumbler (a real breakthrough in hanging basket tomatoes), and Hestia (dwarf climbing bean) have all been superb and are here to stay.

This year, I've strong hopes amongst my new introductions for the Kong series: Coleus,

Millet and Purple Majesty (a stately dot plant) and several of the many new dianthus. Billy Bell is the early exhibition chrysanthemum we are all pinning our hopes on - so far, so good. I was also very impressed with the several new Celosias I saw on trial. They are an old love of mine and are included in my trials.

I've strong hopes amongst my new introductions for the Kong series: Coleus, Millet and Purple Majesty

GARDEN TIPS

- Keep your young plants happy by applying weak liquid fertiliser. Don't be tempted to bed out too early, aim for strong, healthy bushy plants.

- Should you be lucky enough to have lots of greenhouse space, give plenty of room between pots and trays of young plants - this encourages sturdy development.

Celosia: Pink Glow. A superb variety at the trial grounds of Ball Colegrave, near Banbury back in 2004

Mid-April, right in the middle of the daffodil/spring show season. As an exhibitor from way back, I never cease to marvel at the enthusiasm these generate and the sheer skill and dedication they promote - long may it continue.

It is difficult to place a finger on what makes a top prize-winning variety. Suffice to say it must have that magic, indefinable something that makes it stand out from the rest, whether it be fruit, flower or vegetable. Gold Star tomato, Gringo carrot and Billy Bell chrysanthemum immediately spring to mind, but the list is endless.

I never cease to marvel at the enthusiasm that shows generate

GARDEN TIPS

- Are you, like me, finding two seedlings in many plug plants now arriving by post? If so, take my advice and carefully cut off the weakest at soil level. I use a fine pointed pair of scissors.

- Now is the ideal time to visit specialist fuschia nurseries and buy young whips to grow into standards. It's great fun and well worth the challenge.

Past glories from my archives: Superb show-stopping gladioli and chrysanthemums

Not just in my garden, but across the whole of the country, the joys of spring are really evident with both blossom and fragrance. Yes, winter is slowly losing its grip and a new season of growth is emerging - truly enchanting.

My garden is living up to its name - Magnolia Cottage - with countless blooms on my magnolias soulangianas and these are joined in the area with flowering cherries, each awash with vibrant dainty colour and perfume to gladden our hearts.

One so often reads of planting for an all-year-round effect and I strongly subscribe to this. Remember, so many trees and shrubs are compact or erect growers, and so are eminently suitable for the small plot. As a guide, I've listed below a brief selection, with descriptions, of tried and tested spring beauties ideal for this area.

FLOWERING CHERRIES/ALMONDS

PRUNUS AMANOGAWA - upright, columnar growth with pretty pink/white blossom in profusion. Height 10ft.

SHERATON CHERRY KANZAN - double flowered pink blossom with a bonus of shining, polished mahogany winter bark. Will make 12-15ft in height.

PRUNUS SERRULA - May flowering - white again, polished mahogany bark in autumn.

MALUS - ornamental crab apples. Usually follows prunus with their blossom and, unlike prunus, you can get varieties with bright red colour.

MAGNOLIAS

SOULANGIANA - the most widely grown with huge tulip-like blooms, white with a mauve/pink base. Do remember, however, it can make 30ft high and wide.

RUBRA - smaller, deep pink blooms.

STELLATA - often called the star magnolia with white, black-centred star-like flowers.

DWARF - will flower at 3ft high. A small garden must-have!

Appropriate: Magnolia soulangiana in full bloom at Magnolia Cottage

Winter is slowly losing its grip and a new season of growth is emerging - truly enchanting.

GARDEN TIPS

- Replace yellow sticky traps in your greenhouse. Apart from trapping whitefly and other pests, they give a good guide as to what is 'on wing' in your area.

- It is now time to start applying natural predators (nematodes) to our containers to control vine weevil.

SIZE MATTERS IN THE WORLD OF SMASHING PUMPKINS...

My idea of a fun plant is the growing of giant pumpkins - a guaranteed talking point. Imagine, from a tiny flat seed just a quarter of an inch long, planted in April, a monster hernia-inducing giant of up to 300lbs - yes, 300lbs - can be harvested by September. Mind blowing.

I've been growing them with mixed success for many years and never fail to marvel at their growth pattern. As ever, the seed strain is vital, with Atlantic Giant, or its variants, being the main choice.

They should be sown around the end of April, singly, on edge, in a four-inch diameter pot under glass. Being a member of the curcubit family, a fast and regular variety, no check growth pattern is essential.

Plant out in the sunniest site or under a poly tunnel in late May. Put lots of humus in the soil and, once established, water and feed constantly. Liquid feeding is the key to success, plus restricting each plant to one fruit. Hand pollinate and stop the plant at the second pair of leaves after a pumpkin is set and expanding.

Specialist pumpkin shows are usually held in the South – Sheffield's nearest major event is the Soham Pumpkin Fair in Cambridgeshire. This was the venue for the 2006 National Championship, a competition that resrticts entries to pumpkins weighing over 90kgs. Well worth seeing if you've never seen these giants. My heaviest to date, you ask? A mere 78lbs!

The magic world of pumpkins: Don't drop this monster pumpkin on your foot!

PUMPKIN TIPS

- Guard against slugs - they can ruin a prizewinner overnight.

- While the pumpkin is small, carefully and gently move the developing fruit to ensure the stem is in a straight line from the main stem so sap can flow freely. As usual, it's attention to detail that brings success.

STUART'S SWEETCORN SPECIAL

T hanks to growing public demand, the media, and seed breeders' improvements, sweetcorn is fast becoming a national delicacy.

May I pass on my tricks of the trade to ensure success? Firstly, don't start the seed too early. A fast, consistent growth pattern with no checks is vital.

Sow the seed in early May, under cold glass or a coldframe, singly in three inch pots. Plant-out in early June in the warmest, sunniest bed that has been well prepared. Plant in blocks, not rows, as sweetcorn is wind-pollinated, and keep well watered.

The time taken from cropping to eating must be kept to an absolute minimum as the sugar content quickly changes to starch. When are they ready? As the cobs develop, carefully peel back the outer husk of a large cob – still attached to the plant – to expose the rows of pearly seed. Gently press your thumbnail into the seed. If the sap is thin and watery, the corn is not yet ready. If it is as thick as single cream past its best but milky...perfect!

A final tip before cropping: have a pan of boiling water ready on the stove so the cobs can be plunged straight into the water. This may seem like a lot of trouble, but do try it...the end result is pure bliss!

P.S. My apologies to fridge and deep-freeze manufacturers!

The sweetest taste: Transfer straight from garden to pan for the best results

JOBS FOR MAY

BULBS: Lift lilies for decoration and tulips when finished.

COMPOST BINS: Empty your compost bins and use as mulch as May and June are the maximum growth months and lots of new material will be available.

FRUIT: Protect strawberries from late frost.

FLOWER BEDS: There are usually lots of bargains to be had on larger-sized plug plants and single-pot bedders – ideal for cap filling.

ROSES: It's your last opportunity to mulch your rosebeds. Don't forget to watch out for pests!

M A Y

May, in my book, is an 'all systems go' month. Start planting out summer bedding in containers, planters and window boxes. Remember to include in your compost both water-retaining granules and slow-release fertiliser granules (I use a six-month type) – great labour saving products.

If you own a greenhouse, plant tomatoes, cucumbers and peppers in their final pots or growbags. On hot days, ventilate the space well and dampen down your greenhouse path to deter red spider mite.

Talking of pests, don't forget to spray roses against their major problems: blackspot and aphids.

Cut the grass as often as time allows, but be careful not to 'scalp' it. Remember, regular cutting promotes the desired finer grasses; bowling greens are cut every one to two days to maintain perfection.

Towards the end of the month, it should be safe to plant out dahlias, sweetcorn, runner beans and French beans. If in doubt, wait 'til early June.

Lift and dry daffodils and tulips unless you'd rather leave them to naturalise. Store them in paper bags or trays and keep them cool until it's time for September planting.

THE HORTICULTURAL JOKER – A PLANT WITH REAL PURPOSE

I defy anyone to name a plant with more purpose than the horticultural joker - the sunflower. Loved by children of all ages, guaranteed to lift your spirits come rain or shine, no side or snob value, just a joy to both grow and enjoy.

Grown both commercially for its vegetable oil - second only to olive oil in quantity produced - and beloved of sun lovers for the cheerful blooms, sunflowers have quite a noble history. Remember, Oscar Wilde used it as his personal emblem!

Its fast rate of growth makes the sunflower ideal for bringing children into our great hobby; we all know how impatient they can become. Ideal, of course, for school competitions and a great educational starter plant.

Growing them is so simple. As the name implies, sun is their major requirement, coupled with plenty of moisture and a free draining soil. They can be sown direct into the ground in early May. Set two seeds per station and, if both emerge, remove the weakest.

Alternatively, and the method I use, is to sow two seeds in a three inch pot, again discarding the weakest, and plant the best in a prepared spot late May.

Rapid strides in sunflower breeding has taken place in both colour, form and height. Whilst the traditional yellow is the most popular, both commercially and for the monsters, lots of red, bronze, maroon and plum coloured varieties are also available. Heights vary from dwarfs (just a foot or so tall) to monsters towering to 15/18 ft, with Russian Giant being a popular example.

Sunflowers are notorious for producing lots of pollen that can not only stain their petals but your clothing, too. Our breeders have responded by developing pollen-free varieties, such as the red-petalled Starburst Dandy, and Lemon Aura, a lemon-shaded counterpart.

Wildlife and organic gardeners pay due homage to sunflowers, due to their attraction to birds, bees and friendly insects.

Yes, sunflowers are a real fun plant, whether you are nine or ninety, with such a fantastic choice of varieties that really are child's play to grow – honestly!

Wildlife and organic gardeners pay due homage to sunflowers, due to their attraction to birds, bees and friendly insects.

SUNFLOWER TIPS

- Remember, the heads turn to follow the sun, so pick your planting site with care.
- Do stake and tie in plants from an early stage. They are so easily damaged by winds and heavy rain.

Sunny outlook: Part of large trial bed devoted to sunflowers at Sutton's Seeds Ltd in Devon

DAHLIAS BACK IN DEMAND

Yes, we are all human and can, perhaps, be rather smug in an 'I told you so' attitude when our thoughts and ideas come good.

I refer to the dahlia family, which, through no fault of its own, has been in something of a wilderness in the last decade or so, at least with the home gardener, although the show growers still hold their own.

Public thoughts can be rather fickle but I do believe the resurgence of the dahlia can be traced to one variety - the Bishop of Llandaff - which has received incredible publicity. Yes, it is a cracker, with its vibrant red colour set off by great dark foliage and stems, and yet as old as the hills! Such is the power of the press!

For a vast choice of colour, shape, form and height, dahlias truly are your oyster - you name it and it's available. Size ranges from tiny poms (two inches in diameter) to giants as big as dinner plates. Shapes ranging from the spiky cacti-type and water lily form, to the decorative and single open dwarf bedding types are all available. All have several things in common. Firstly originating from South America they are frost tender, so defer planting out till early June, and all will make underground tubers for lifting and drying in autumn.

Dahlias can be bought in two formats, as dormant tubers or, from specialist sources, green plants, that is, cuttings taken from sprouted tubers and rooted. Dormant tubers are usually sold in a polythene bag with coloured pictures and growing instructions. These can be either potted up and placed in a frost-free greenhouse to shoot or planted directly into your garden, but do guard against frost. Early May is quite early enough for the Sheffield area – the further north you are, the later you should leave it.

I believe the resurgence of the dahlia can be traced to one variety - the Bishop of Llandaff

They require sun, plus lots of water. Remember, in a few short months they make large clumps with many flowers. Truly a cut and come again flower. Soft stems do require staking but are so rewarding. Yes, I agree, the flowers have a short vase life but worry not, another bunch will quickly appear, I promise.

Aphids and earwigs are their prime enemies. Spray against aphids, and for earwigs the time honoured trick is to crumple up some tissue paper or soft straw, place in an empty three inch plant pot, invert this and hang on a cane used to support your dahlia plants. Empty daily of earwigs and dispose of these as you choose.

DAHLIA TIPS

- The Sheffield area has some great dahlia shows, always in September. Do try to visit these to see the vast range available.

- When growing for cut flowers, take a jug of water to your dahlia bed. Cut and plunge stems immediately into water. Remember, dahlias are hollow stemmed and can wilt due to an air lock if not instantly placed in water.

Dahlias: A mid-summer spectacle now back in vogue

STAND BY YOUR BEDS AND GET A REWARDING DISPLAY

Yes - it's all go in the big works! Here we are very much at the summer bedding out time with not a moment to spare.

I always compare summer bedding displays with a craftsman painting a house – 90% of the time is spent on preparation; 10% in applying the paint.

Our beds and borders should have been rough dug in the winter and welded, and should now be raked to a fine tilth ready to provide a snug home for all our summer flowering treasures. Incorporate in the top inch or so a dressing of fish, blood and bone or chicken manure pellets at approximately 4oz per sq yd to give a steady food supply.

As the drill sergeant stated, plant with the tallest at the back and shortest at the front in a bed or border, or in the case of a circular bed, tallest in the centre. Plant firmly and remember that plants grow, so allow space for them to develop. Water in, stand back and enjoy.

Routine watering and deadheading should be carried out on a regular basis.

Ideas, methods and plants change, and one recent development is the move to shorter, compact ranges suitable for smaller beds, containers and even window boxes. Such subjects as delphiniums, larkspur, sunflowers, lupins and chrysanthemums are now being miniaturised. This is quite an emotive issue for, whilst I can see a need for this, the joy of tall, fully grown plants takes some beating. Frankly, the thought of a sunflower dwarfed say to nine inches in height is not my cup of tea. But then, each to his own.

After all the time, trouble and expense taken in bedding out, it is obviously sad to see pests ravage our displays. Slugs, snails, vine weevil and aphids are our major problems. Nematodes/natural predators are very much in vogue, but the choice of attack must be yours.

It amazes me how attitudes change, not that I wish to be controversial. The RSPB, after years of claiming that slug pellets put garden birds at risk, have now admitted there is no evidence of a single bird being killed. They state it is Britain's eight million cats that kill 55 million birds each year. Who counts them, I ask? By the way, for the record, I'm a cat lover!

A good idea with some of our slightly tender specialist plants, such as phormiums, cordylines, abutilons and hibiscus, is to pot grow them then sink - pot and all - into our beds to give instant cover. Lift in the autumn and return to a greenhouse.

BEDDING OUT TIPS

- Water plants well 24 hours before bedding out then water again after planting.

- When buying plants, go for the ones just coming into bud rather than those in full colour. Half the fun is watching them develop.

Massed beds: Time to put in work for the summer to get a good display

LEGUMES MEANS BEANS – AND DON'T FORGET PEAS, TOO!

*I*t was with eager anticipation I spent time this week weeding and stopping my earliest planted broad beans, which are now in full flower. The black/white flowers - quite attractive in their own right - are hopefully a forerunner of feasts to come.

As often mentioned, nothing can compare with the taste of really fresh fruit and veg and the news from the trade is that veg seeds/plants have this year really soared. Great news for, apart from the freshness, do bear in mind we amateurs grow varieties firstly for taste, not quantity.

Legumes - the bean/pea family - are to many one of the most popular ranges of veg and grow well in the Sheffield area. Broad beans and peas are quite hardy, but French and runner beans are frost tender. With our rather short frost-free growing season - usually June to late September - these are best sown under glass, either in a coldframe or greenhouse, and planted out when all risk of frost has passed.

In the past, I've always sown these singly in small pots or cell trays but this year I've changed to root trainers which gave me a long, straight, superb root structure.

A fairly new type of bean is the dwarf/bush climbing bean - hestia being a great example. Growing to a height of only 2ft or so, it performs well in a container when trained up a wigwam of canes – it looks great with pretty red/white flowers festooning the pyramid with beans to follow.

Freshness cannot be overemphasised and regular cropping every four to five days is essential to ensure a long season.

Homegrown garden peas are a delicacy not to be missed. They are best grown in rows and sown directly two inches deep. A good tip to ensure full rows is to sow a few extra, two or three peas to a three-inch pot, as 'spares' to fill in any gaps. Apart from neatness, it ensures a full crop.

One fascinating feature of all members of the legume plant family is their inbuilt ability to extract nitrogen from the air. This is transferred to the roots where it appears as tiny white spheres. At the end of the season, it is best to turn these into the soil as 'free' nitrogen.

From the foregoing, you will realise that fertilisers for legumes should be high in phosphates and potash and low in nitrogen. Water retentive soil is ideal.

Enjoy your legumes!

LEGUME TIPS

- The old tip of lining pea/bean trenches with old water soaked newspapers is great to hold in essential moisture.

- To encourage runner beans to set, try the old established method of placing amongst your rows jars of sugar water - they attract bees and pollinating insects.

A good crop: Young, greenhouse raised broad bean plants all ready for planting out

JOBS FOR JUNE

LAWNS: Apply summer weed feed and moss killer (water in during dry spells).

BULBS: Water gladioli during dry spells.

BEDDING: Plant summer bedding and sow spring flowering biennials. Dead-heading will pay great dividends later in the year.

VEGETABLE PATCH: Nip out broad bean shoots.

FRUIT: Mulch strawberries.

GREENHOUSE: Put on summer shading to keep the area cool.

ROSES: Apply summer fertiliser, hoe, mulch, spray and water as required.

JUNE

A month to really enjoy the wonders of gardening and all it entails. Balmy days, long evenings, and with most of the planting done, a time to relax on a warm evening with a glass of 'falling-down water'! Back to gardening...

For vegetable growers, plant sweetcorn out in blocks, not rows, as it is wind-pollinated. Plant pumpkins on well-prepared sites enriched with lots of compost. Don't forget, they love lots of water and room to grow. Plant-out your winter greens (i.e. sprouts, winter cabbage, cauliflower and broccoli), and sow swedes – a superb and much underrated Autumn vegetable.

Roses... this is their special month. After flowering, cut-back each flowered stem by at least a foot to promote a second flush in August/September. Help this along by giving them a top dressing of fertiliser and spray once again against blackspot and aphids.

Keep mowing! And don't forget to trim lawn edges - it'll make such a difference to the overall appearance of your garden. Keep hoeing, too – this is the month that the Dutch hoe comes into its own for weed control. If time is at a premium, remember that glyphosate weed killer is totally safe, but do apply strictly as instructed. I keep a special sprayer just for this.

After a summer storm or heavy rainfall, dash out and apply a mulch of at least two inches (three inches is even better) around shrubs, bushes and trees to conserve moisture. This both controls weeds and encapsulates precious water.

ON BLUEBERRY HILL

Yes, we can all reminisce, and nostalgia is a great source of memories from yesteryear.

The most interest shown today in soft fruit, judging by my post bag and phone calls, is in blueberries. They are widely extolled by health food gurus and nutritionalists, but when I think of blueberries my mind immediately goes back to my teenage years and a smash hit song, the immortal Fats Domino with Blueberry Hill.

It is quite amazing how blueberries have taken off in popularity in the last few years but, if one delves a little into this plant, it is easy to understand why. Blueberries are closely related to bilberries and these grow wild in many spots around Sheffield, giving a crop in August/September, and make great pies, either combined with apple or on their own.

When one considers their natural habitat, i.e. moorland/heather-strewn areas of very low pH, it follows that the cultivated blueberry needs to be grown in ericaceous compost with a pH of 5.0/5.5 (totally lime-free).

Blueberries make ideal container plants, being fully hardy, and they offer so much with flowers, superb fruit and, as a bonus, red autumn/winter colour - beat that!

To achieve maximum pollination, it is strongly advised that you grow two distinct varieties and I often suggest a pair as focal points on your patio or flanking your front porch. They make for a great talking point and could be real trend setters.

Popular: Blueberries have really taken off in the last few years

It is quite amazing how blueberries have taken off in popularity in the last few years

Use large containers, 2ft wide and deep, with plenty of drainage holes and well crocked. Use John Innes No. 3 Ericaceous Compost for long life and stability.

Feed with an ericaceous type liquid fertiliser from March to August, and an annual dressing of sequestered iron or iron sulphate is well worthwhile.

SOFT FRUIT TIPS

- Try growing blueberries in one of the many raised beds now available, filled with ericaceous compost.

- Spray gooseberries now against American mildew and gooseberry sawfly caterpillar.

No thorns, compact growth, easy to crop; just lightly prune to shape in early spring and replace the top two to three inches of compost with fresh compost every two years. All in all, a great doer – so fill your boots!

P.S. When berries turn blue wait at least a further seven days as they will both swell and sweeten. Suggested varieties - Bluecrop, Herbert, Chandler, Polaris and Goldtraube 71.

A SWARD OF HONOUR

arly June, and with a little luck, we should start to see our reward for all the spring planning and effort. Our beds and borders should all be planted, hanging baskets and containers developing nicely...so what else remains to demand our attention? Yes, the lawn.

It is often said, but not always heeded, that the lawn is the most overworked yet most neglected part of our garden. Whilst one must not become a slave to our 'grass patch' it is, nevertheless, true that grass responds quickly to a little TLC.

The lawn is the most overworked yet most neglected part of our garden.

The amount of grass removed by regular mowing in a season is quite staggering so replacing nutrients is of paramount importance. With modern lawn care products and, for a medium/larger lawn, a spreader to facilitate applying them, feeding a lawn takes only minutes.

Slow release fertilisers give months of steady nutrients so a spring feed (high in nitrogen) followed by an autumn application of a high potash formulation should give good results.

Regular mowing is the most important need; at least every seven days from May to September should be the aim. It keeps coarser grasses in check, promoting a much better finish. Never

scalp a lawn and, in drought conditions, leave the grass box off so that the clippings act as a mulch. Scarifying and hollow tining at least twice per year promotes healthier grass by allowing the ingress of life-giving oxygen and detering the build-up of moss and thatch.

Finally, edging your lawn after mowing gives a finished look and sets the seal for your garden. There are no short cuts to a good lawn other than regular attention, but the selection of good equipment, i.e. mower, lawn edging shears, fertiliser, etc, are all sound investments and should lighten your workload.

When laying a new lawn - whether turf or seed - preparation is of paramount importance and should not be hurried. Both turf and seed are available in many qualities. Select with care and do shop around. If possible, see a finished lawn.

I am often asked why grass seed germinates erratically, so here's a simple proven tip. Chill the seed in your fridge and wait for a warm day to sow. The rapid change in temperature jolts it into even germination. Not a lot of people know that!

Enjoy your lawn!

A sound investment: Look after your lawn and reap the rewards

LAWN TIPS

- Change your direction of mowing every third or fourth cut as this stimulates the grass.

- For a quick 'green-up', apply a high nitrogen liquid fertiliser. A hose end applicator makes this a simple operation and the results are quickly visible.

BIG, BRASH AND BEAUTIFUL – YOU CAN'T MISS A COLEUS

I am including in my spotlight this week a plant solely due to the lasting impression it made on me at my first sighting. This incredible range of Coleus plant was released in 2005 under the name Kong.

The blue flower spikes are quite insignificant but the multicoloured, near garish giant foliage makes them totally mind blowing.

The Kong range of plants beggars description; whilst it is a member of that popular foliage family, Coleus, its size is simply sensational. Modern plant breeders are known for their versatility and achievement, but these are so dramatic they almost appear to be fed with horticultural steroids! Each leaf can easily reach nine inches in length by five inches wide and the brilliant colours really leap out at you.

The range is comprised of five colours, namely, red, green, rose, scarlet and mosaic, each with its own individual markings and charm. These were one of the highlights at the press day of Ball Colgrave near Banbury, who assured us that the plants are quite hardy enough to be used outside (summer months, of course) in containers or border displays.

As with all Coleus, the blue flower spikes are quite insignificant but the multicoloured, near garish giant foliage make them totally mind blowing.

Coleus have always been a good, reliable foliage plant. I well remember Rotherham Corporation Nurseries making a regular feature of the aptly named variety Paisley Shawl in the '60s and '70s but this Kong series is a complete breakthrough.

*You'll either love 'em or hate
'em, but one thing is for sure,
you certainly can't ignore them!*

Bright idea: Coleus Kong, the new range of plants

Yes, you'll either love 'em or hate 'em, but one thing is for sure, you certainly can't ignore them!

P.S. Plant out in June in good light to enhance the vivid colours and wear sunglasses!

GARDEN TIPS

- Roses have suffered badly this year with black spot. Clear up all fallen leaves and give a final spray with Rose Clear 3 or similar to destroy any spores.

- Lift early chrysanthemum stools and place in a greenhouse or coldframe. Keep on the dry side until New Year.

A PERENNIAL BEAUTY

The season for outdoor entertaining is upon us, the time when we can get full benefit from the 'outdoor room'. One group of plants, perennials, can help to deliver results that you can be proud of whilst still allowing plenty of deckchair time.

Perennials are so versatile that many will thrive in pots and containers on paved patios, balconies and roof gardens. Emerging every spring, they grow up quickly in the rising temperatures and by June many are already flowering, bringing joyful colour. As well as beautiful flowers, many have attractive foliage too. If space is limited, it's important to choose plants that deliver in more than one way, or over a longer time span, resulting in maximum ornamental value.

Some of the best perennials, in my opinion, include: achillea (known as yarrow), aquilegia (columbine) and digitalis (foxglove).

Achillea - these are perfect in wild flower or rock gardens; their daisy-like flowers giving a naturalistic feel. Taller varieties are perfect for borders and their gorgeous colours range from bright reds and yellows to blush pinks and soft whites - lots of choice, whatever your colour scheme. There's an added bonus, too, as they are some of the best perennials for cutting and drying, so if you're feeling creative, you can enjoy them inside and out! I suggest achillea millefolium - brilliant yellow blooms consisting of tiny florets with aromatic green-grey leaves.

Aquilegia - these clump-forming perennials are ideal for herbaceous borders and self-seed like fury. Look out for aquilegia chrysantha with its eye-catching yellow flowers. Aquilegia vulgaris varieties are reliable and come in shades of deep violet, pink and white. Nora Barlow is a favourite, producing beautiful pink and greenish-white flowers on strong leafy stems.

Digitalis - foxgloves are real classics. Again, self-seed and come in many truly pretty shades, with speckles and contrasting tones. Many new varieties are widely available.

All of the above are fully hardy and do not normally require a lot of care. Tidy up at the end of the flowering season, cutting back dead or withered shoots and weed at the same time. Water in dry spells, though a good mulch will minimise the need for this, and feed each spring with a slow release fertiliser.

There is a growing trend to grow more perennials as labour savers and just fill in gaps with the brightest low growing bedding plants, such as impatiens, petunias, gazanias, etc. Well worth considering for next year.

GARDEN TIPS

- Delphiniums/lupins - cut back quite hard as blooms fade. Give a light dressing base fertiliser. After a hot summer, a second flowering can be yours September/October.

- Greenhouse tomatoes - stop these at the next pair of leaves after the fourth or fifth truss is formed. This will speed ripening.

Beautiful blooms: Perennials in full glory

JOBS FOR JULY

Weeding, feeding and, if dry, watering are the essential tasks.

LAWNS: A liquid, high nitrogen feed will give a quick green-up to our lawns.

VEGETABLE PATCH: Earth up main crop potatoes and sow a last sowing of stump rooted carrots and baby beetroot for an October harvest.

GREENHOUSE: Water, feed and tie up tomatoes, cucumbers and peppers. Stop tomatoes in a cold greenhouse after the fifth truss is formed.

FLOWER BEDS/CONTAINERS. Look out for cheap end of season bedding plants to fill any gaps that may occur. Stand out tender plants such as orchids on really hot days, to enjoy a mini holiday.

JULY

High summer – a month when so much of our earlier work comes to fruition. Watering, weeding and dead-heading are our main tasks, but do visit as many open gardens as possible (main requirements: notebook and pencil!).

This is very much a 'between seasons' time for our beloved hobby and industry. Nurseries and garden centres are usually only ticking over until the Autumn rush. It's a good time to snap-up bargains in base materials such as compost and sundries. Even major items like garden furniture, power tools and greenhouses are on offer as the new season models appear in a few weeks and space is at a premium.

Enjoy your fruit and veg; remember to pick young and aim to beat the world record in time taken from 'plant to plate'. With vegetables, the quicker the better for maximum flavour. Speaking of vegetables, it's your last chance to sow peas, carrots and French beans for a late autumn feast.

Now is a good time to take cuttings of semi-ripe young shoots of many hardy shrubs – a coldframe is an ideal home for them. You should also be de-budding bloom chrysanthemums to encourage September flowers – and keep them well tied to their canes.

Check any spring bulbs you have in store to ensure their soundness. A further dusting of sulphur powder is beneficial.

Lastly, visit some summer shows and note the successful varieties that repeat around the country – remember, they have that special in-built magic that makes them stand out.

A ROOM WITH A VIEW

It is an obvious suggestion, and one actively acted on, that apart from being an outdoor activity, gardeners spend so much so-called 'leisure time' outdoors.

The theme is to create and use your garden as an extension to your home and literally plan part as extra rooms. The possibilities are virtually endless - whether you want to build a tiny private hideaway or an open plan dining area.

Screening off areas of the garden can create a sense of mystery and intrigue and provide a private corner in which to while away lazy summer days - gardening tasks permitting!

Designing your garden around a single structure, such as a pergola, is an elegant and easy way to transform your outdoor living space, while also creating a focal point. I often suggest we grow upwards, after all, height is usually unlimited, and our choice of climbers for a pergola is quite bewildering. Wood is a natural material so sympathetic to plants and, correctly treated, will last for many years and blend in with our plantings.

Strong emphasis should be placed on perfume - after all, plant fragrance is a must to any true plantsman. Be adventurous in your choice, and remember: climbing roses, honeysuckles and clematis can intertwine, so creating an ever-changing vista.

To enhance your pergola, may I make a suggestion of including containers containing the old cottage garden favourites of night scented stocks and lavenders to give perfume to die for?

Many of the newer forms of lavender are truly exotic, both in form and scent, and make ideal container subjects for your secret outdoor room. Amongst the newer varieties Lavender Lace and Lilac Wings are true treasures, giving all that is best in grace, colour and perfume - seek 'em out! My favourite white is Lavender Snowman, which makes a great container plant and, being white, a really cool subject.

Yes, whether as a private place to unwind and watch the garden world drift by, or as a major focal point, do consider a pergola - perhaps best of all as your own secret special corner to dream your private dreams.

P.S. The addition of a small water feature would really create a Shangri-La. Remember, the sound/movement of water is so peaceful and calming.

GARDEN TIPS

- Pumpkins/marrows - If you're growing the biggies for the shows, give lots of liquid feed and water - they really are hungry and thirsty plants.

- Coleus Kong - Take my tip and take out the flower stem as it emerges. Remember, it's grown for the fantastic foliage, not the flower.

Pergolas: For poise, privacy and perfume

LIVE LIFE ON THE HEDGE

Architectural shapes, focal points and bold statements are oft repeated phrases by the gardening media when discussing garden designs and planning. Topiary, an ancient craft, is now enjoying quite a revival and is well worthy of a closer study.

Clipped forms and shapes of box and yew have long been prominent in stately and formal homes and gardens but can be just as effective in the tiniest of gardens and even as home or conservatory potted focal points.

Small leafed ivy makes a simple, cheap and quick growing starter plant when used in a terracotta pot. Ideally, start with two young plants in a seven- or eight-inch terracotta pot planted centrally. Take a metal coat hanger and form this into a heart shape with a central straight leg six- to eight-inches long inserted behind the two young ivy plants. As they grow, train up either side of the heart shape, holding them in place with sweet pea rings.

For outdoor containers, box is by far the favourite, due to its compact, small leaf growth pattern, with yew a close second and more suitable for larger forms.

Privet, in particular the golden type, was widely used in my early days as a cheap, quick growing alternative, but has now been, in the main, superseded.

Specialist sources for both ready-formed plants and starter kits are available and topiary is now widely featured at most major garden shows.

A word in hedgeways: A topiary display at Harrogate Spring Show, 2005

GARDEN TIPS

- When pruning try not to cut leaves in half - it can be a source of entry for various diseases

- Use John Innes No. 3 compost for all containers used for long-term topiary.

COMPOSTING: YOU KNOW IT MAKES SENSE

Yes, composting is good for you, good for the environment, good for your soil and plants and, above all, will give you a real feeling of self-satisfaction. I often feel that one of the main reasons people are put off making their own garden compost is the vision of the old allotment sites with piles of rotting plant debris. In fact, nothing could be further from the truth. Let us consider compost, composting and the benefits.

We gardening gurus glibly talk about rich soil and impoverished soils but, basically, the key word is "humus". Humus, so the dictionary tells us, is defined as follows: "a complex entity of the soil arising from the decomposition of organic matter, the vital residue of plant food" - in short, the basis of soil fertility. This says it all; so where do we start?

Compost making is simple and should be continuous but needs a little care and attention. A rectangular shaped bin is best, situated in a semi shaded spot and covered with either black polythene or old carpet to help retain heat.

All vegetative matter can be composted, such as 'soft' weeds, decaying plants, grass cuttings, veg and fruit waste, egg shells, cardboard (shredded), newspaper (not glossy), light prunings - the list is endless. Items to avoid include fish and meat waste (which can attract vermin), tough perennial weeds, such as docks, dandelions, creeping buttercups, bindweed, etc, as our weather does not tend to generate enough heat to destroy these.

Air is a vital ingredient to assist the degrading process, so build your heap in layers and mix as you go. Try to avoid too much of one type. Grass cuttings should be interspersed with light, twiggy prunings to admit air.

Composting should build up heat. This encourages microbial activity to break down the bulk. An activator, either powder or liquid, certainly helps to speed up the process. Compost should not be allowed to dry, so water if necessary. Conversely, if it becomes over wet, add crumpled up newspapers or, better still, shredded cardboard. For the smaller garden, don't despair if you feel you haven't the space. Some good quality, small and neat bins, containers and rotary drums are available, and these can easily be masked for appearance's sake with a planted container or two. Rotary drums are very effective and produce quality compost quickly. A wormery is a small intriguing method that also produces liquid fertiliser as a bonus to the compost.

Remember, well-made garden compost is free yet in nutrient value richer than the best FYM.

So, how to use it? There are many uses, such as a mulch, digging into your beds and borders, to conserve moisture and suppress weeds, lining your pea and bean trenches - the list just goes on. Remember, a humus-rich soil is so receptive to the fertilisers you may apply, in other words, the fertiliser will feed your plants and not the soil.

How long does it take to make good compost? It all depends on the time of year, but the

Correx compost bin

longer you leave it, the better it becomes. Ideally, you should have two containers/heaps, one you are making, one you are using.

Comfrey is a plant so often associated with composting on two counts. Firstly, the leaves stewed make great high potash liquid fertiliser and secondly, leaves added to your compost act as a super activator. Make a note of the variety Bocking 14, which I find is the best.

So many of our local and regional councils have taken up the importance of composting by supplying bins and containers either free of charge or at a very attractive price. I've been involved in many of these schemes and commend them to you.

So, go on, have a go - you know it makes sense!

GARDEN TIPS

- Remember thick, fleshy leaf plants are far more drought tolerant than the thin leafed varieties.

- In hot spells, remove grass box from your mower and leave the mowings as a mulch.

SPRING STARTS HERE WHEN ORDERING UP YOUR BULBS

Yes, it really does. Whilst we are still enjoying our summer flowers and veg, spare a thought - at least for planning and ordering – for next spring. Now is the time when keen gardeners, in particular the exhibiting fraternity, are ordering bulbs to, hopefully, give success and a great display.

The colour and perfume are a great tonic in the darkest winter days

The best advice I can give is to plan ahead and compile a buying list of your requirements. Remember, the early bird catches the worm, for many of the choicest varieties sell out quickly. Christmas flowering hyacinths take approximately 14-16 weeks from potting to perfection, so one can appreciate fairly prompt action needs to be taken if these are on your list. Frankly, though, with all the many visual Christmas attractions, I personally subscribe to January flowering for them, when the colour and perfume are a great tonic in the darkest winter days.

The 'ordinary', or garden, hyacinths are superb in containers as a centrepiece in a mixed dwarf bulb display adding colour and perfume and are amazingly long lasting - at their best in late March/early April.

When considering bulb plantings don't forget your hanging baskets. Whilst our summer baskets should be a great item, the ones in spring really stand out as a warm welcome over your porch. The choice for winter/spring baskets is really wide-ranging, from all the dwarf bulbs like daffs, tulips, crocus and iris, to winter flowering pansies like heathers, bellis, etc.

Should you have a selection of baskets and containers, I often mass just one variety to make a bold statement. When selecting bulbs, check for a firm base and go for the largest size depending on species. In beds and borders, planting depth is important but so many amateurs do not plant deeply enough. Two to three times the bulb's height is a good guide, and plant as soon as summer bedding fades and the area is cleared and fertilised. A dressing of Vitax Q4 or fish, blood and bone gives good results, and a light dusting of sulphate of potash in late February improves colour and stem strength no end.

So, even though it's still summer, take time out to plan for next spring. No rest for the wicked!

GARDEN TIPS

- Outdoor cyclamen corms are usually on sale in September. They love a semi-shaded spot. Plant, leave to multiply and enjoy!

- Mixed daffs can be disappointing due to different flowering dates. It's better to buy distinct varieties and plant in bold clumps.

Planning ahead: Hyacinths make a good show - order your bulbs for next year

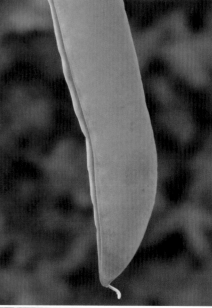

JOBS FOR AUGUST

LAWNS: Cut regularly. If dry, leave grass box off.

FRUIT: Harvest when ripe, destroying damaged fruit. Prune plums as needed, cutting out crossing branches.

VEGETABLE PATCH: Lift crops when young to use or freeze. Plant out spring cabbage/winter broccoli. Spray main crop potatoes against blight (I use Dithane 945).

GREENHOUSE: Stop tomatoes, cucumbers and peppers to hasten ripening.

FLOWER BORDERS: Compost spent flowers, keep hoeing against weeds. Replant daffodils and narcissi. Work in bonemeal/fish, blood and bone before planting.

DAHLIAS/CHRYSANTHEMUMS/GLADIOLI: Keep well staked and cut as ready.

SPRING BULBS: Early autumn catalogues are out. Order your spring bulbs, choice varieties sell out fast.

AUGUST

❦

This month and next are very much the show season; for many the culmination of a season's work. Yes, we all think we've got better specimens back home than the prize-winners, but just remember the Yorkshire saying, "put up or shut up!"

Do try to enter your local shows – once you've dipped your toe in the water you'll become a better, more knowledgeable grower.

Remember the golden rule though: be a good loser. After all, there can only be one first prize-winner. Always bear in mind, whether growing for showing or just for the sheer joy of it, that winning strains have so much going for them that any regular national prize-winning variety must be good enough for your humble patch.

I urge readers to talk to the winning exhibitors – they are only too pleased to offer help and advice, and, above all, encouragement.

Take cuttings of hydrangeas and hybrid tea and floribunda roses towards the end of the month. Take non-flowering cuttings approximately 1 foot long and plant nine inches deep in a sheltered spot. Dip the base in rooting hormone powder prior to inserting, plant firmly and water in well. It takes six to nine months to root and if only 50% root, consider this a success – after all, remember they are 'freebies'!

GOING FOR BOLD

Colourful, reliable, varied, appealing, long established, these are all adjectives that apply to the annual Bakewell Show. By a tenuous link they can also be applied to my flower genera for August, namely hardy geraniums.

Yes, hardy geraniums are such a wonderful plant family that give a tremendous, long-lived carpet of colour with so few faults and vices. They are such easy 'doers' that we probably take them for granted, but they are certainly worth more than a second glance.

They are seldom listed or referred to as a ground cover plant, but I cannot overstate their use for this purpose - not that they are unworthy of a place of honour in their own right as specimen items.

Not to be confused with the bright, often multicoloured frost tender geraniums (pelargoniums), so popular for summer bedding, the hardy types are virtually vice-free and, once established, will spread rapidly. May I also add that they suffer very little from the ravages of pests and diseases, so you will readily appreciate my enthusiasm.

Geraniums are wonderful allies in the garden, producing beautiful flowers in large quantities - they are true classics of the British summer garden. Like other perennials, they are quick to establish and with limited maintenance they will keep their vigour for years.

One special geranium to look out for is Patricia. Patricia was chosen as international perennial of the year for 2004 by the International Perennial Association and with good reason, as it is an absolute glory. It has a long flowering period, producing magenta pink blooms with dark centres right through the summer.

The smaller, hardy geraniums are great in rock gardens or at the front of borders or sink gardens. Geranium Ann Folkard produces pretty magenta coloured flowers with black centres from midsummer to mid-autumn. If space allows, it can reach a spread of 3ft or more.

Kashmir White produces delicate, refined, saucer-shaped white flowers from early to late summer. Nimbus is another notable choice, with its blue veined petals and fine foliage.

In terms of maintenance, cut back summer's growth in autumn to encourage next year's growth. Splitting clumps every two or three years will also help to rejuvenate plants.

Perennials, like geraniums, are the seasonal stars of gardens all around the country at the moment. They add bold splashes of colour and fun wherever you make space for them. Why not go into the garden today and see where you could introduce some eye-catchers of your own?

GARDEN TIPS

- Lawns - often looking a little tired at this time of year, give an instant green-up by giving a liquid feed of a high nitrogen analysis.

- Runner beans - should now be coming to their peak - remember to crop every 2/3 days to ensure a long season. Keep well watered - it's essential.

An absolute glory: Geranium Patricia with old English roses in the background

REFLECTING ON GARDENING NOW AND IN THE FUTURE

The buzzword on so many lips at the minute is minimalist gardening, not music to my ears as a plantsman!

However, the facts are that global warming is with us and we must adapt our gardens accordingly. Weather patterns are changing with wetter, windier winters and near drought conditions in summer. Consider your own patch.

Here we are, in mid-August and so many of our bedders and containers are fading fast. Rudbeckias, normally associated with September/October are in full bloom, likewise chrysanthemums and dahlias.

I feel to counteract this we should consider earlier planting - maybe with horticultural fleece used against late frosts - in other words, raising plants/plugs earlier. Humus, my favourite buzzword, should be the main ingredient of our soils.

Producing vegetative compost should be a must and I'm delighted that so many of our councils are supporting this with both reclamation sites and offers on composting bins/drums, something I've been very involved in over the years.

When one considers that an average two-bed terraced house can produce 12,000 gallons of rain water from its roof each year, mostly running to waste, may I make a personal plea to these authorities to spend more time and money on water storing and recycling equipment? To store this for the inevitable summer drought should, and must, be a priority.

A minimalist garden can be both attractive and labour-saving. The use of hard landscaping, in other words decking, gravel, cobbles and slate ensures this.

No stone unturned: A local gravel garden. Note the use of foliage plants and grasses

Don't despair, plants will still be essential, but choose with care. Consider types where the leaves are not so vulnerable to water loss, such as sedums, cranesbill, cistus, etc, and to make a bold statement, phormiums, cordylines, bamboos and agapanthus are ideal.

Plant trees that are drought tolerant both for shade and shelter. Mulching should be a top priority.

ROSE BY ANY OTHER NAME WOULDN'T SELL AS WELL...

Vast sums are paid to the advertising industry to evolve brand names that capture the consumer's imagination and embellish the product. The gardening industry is no exception to this.

Without any question, the number one selling base fertiliser in the UK is Growmore, which evolved early in World War Two by Her Majesty's Government as an industry standard and which is still going strong.

It is totally chemical with an analysis of 7/7/7 and originally named National Growmore - yes, that dates me! The product, I suggest, is a big seller because its name is simply a plain statement of fact with no frills. A reminder of those austere days.

After the cessation of hostilities came that grand HT rose, Peace. Yes, a great performer, but how much of its success is due to its name? Also at that time came the potato, Home Guard, which conjures up more wartime memories.

Roses lend themselves well to special names: Eternally Yours, Golden Memories and Golden Wedding sell themselves, and the name Fragrant Cloud does just as the name implies. Ground cover roses are all the rage with Flower Carpet the number one choice. A great performer, with the name saying it all. Would it sell as well if the name was Bill Bloggs, I wonder?

Hanging basket tomatoes are much in vogue with the top three being Tumbler, Tumbling Tom Red and Tumbling Tom Yellow. So descriptive and factual.

Exhibition veg strains also use descriptive titles such as Show Perfection, still the best available variety of garden pea, and Showmaster, a stalwart among onions and probably the best from sets. For the runner bean grower, Long As Your Arm and Enorma are truly descriptive.

Leaving my favourite flower, chrysanthemums, till last, Show Maker is a great strain of dwarf 'mums' for container work, offering a great colour range and, as the name implies, they make a great show. However, among the large show blooms, the Riley family of Woolley Moor, near Alfreton, reigned supreme for many years. So many family names were used, like Karen Riley and Grace Riley, but probably the best known - and still a banker - is Max Riley, a true champion. Not a lot of people know that it was named after Chris Riley's dog, Max!

While writing this I have a glass of falling down water to hand, namely Whisky Mac, a favourite of mine. Incidentally, Whisky Mac is also the name of a bronze HT rose bred by that flamboyant rose guru, Harry Wheatcroft.

What's in a name? Quite a lot by the looks of it!

GARDEN TIPS

- Among daffodils, look out for the aptly named Unique, a show-stopping double, and Strines, a great yellow with a local name.

- Find That Rose, published annually, gives lots of information about names, places, events, anniversaries, etc.

What's in a name? Show Perfection, garden pea, so well named

ATTRACTED TO SHADY CHARACTER

Hostas, predominantly a foliage plant, are in a class of their own because of their fantastic range of colours, leaf shape and form.

They are highly prized by flower arrangers and, whilst noted for their foliage, do produce attractive summer flowers. To provide a taste of just how great the choice is, consider the range of shapes and colours that leaves can be. Heart shaped, ovate, rounded or lance shaped, green, yellow, grey-blue, variegated - all are options.

The different members of the Hosta family have many uses in the modern garden. As clump-forming perennials, they are excellent ground cover plants. They work well in mixed herbaceous borders and some are suitable for planting near water. Smaller species and varieties are excellent for rock gardens or as container plants. They are shade tolerant and will do well under deep-rooted deciduous trees.

Hostas are fully winter-hardy but locate them out of the way of cold winds that could dry them out. In terms of soil, moisture is important, but soils should also be well drained. Their enemies, particularly in spring when the young foliage emerges, are slugs and snails.

Hostas have their own National Society, which speaks volumes of their popularity. Contact The British Hostas and Hemerocallis Society, (R. Bowden), at Cleave House, Sticklepath, Okehampton, Devon, EX20 2NL.

The charming Hosta: An aristocrat amongst plants

GARDEN TIPS

Damp down greenhouse paths to deter spider mite and increase humidity. Use 'grey' water for this - i.e. bath water/washing-up water.

Don't water lawns - leave mowings as a mulch. They will recover, I promise, once the autumn rains arrive.

JOBS FOR SEPTEMBER

LAWNS: Adjust the cutting height of your mower to a minimum of 1.5 inches.

FLOWER BORDERS: Keep late flowering bedding plants dead-headed as necessary.

GREENHOUSE: Clear out tomatoes and cucumbers as they finish; and start potting early bulbs.

FRUIT: Remove all spent raspberry canes, tidy up strawberry beds, and order new fruit plants as needed.

VEGETABLE PATCH: Clear all crops as ready and rough dig lime if necessary.

SEEDS/PLUG PLANTS: New seed and plug plant catalogues are issued this month. Be first and order in bulk with friends as a good cost saving for delivery early next year. Seed potatoes should be ordered now as 'first earlies' will need potting in December/January.

SEPTEMBER

A golden month, a month when my number one flower – the early-bloom Chrysanthemum – comes to perfection. This is the plant that originally fired my imagination and started my horticultural journey.

Tracey Waller was the first major breakthrough in the late '50s of early-bloom chrysanthemum, and really set the seal for us. It is still grown to this day and continues to be referred to amongst 'chrysant' men.

My number one suggestion for autumn garden colour in beds and borders is the cone family, Rudbeckia and Echinacea. Rudbeckias, in particular, are a great family with true autumn shades of gold and bronze, both as HHA and perennials.

They give off their best right through September and October and come in a wide range of heights and colours. As a bonus, they make a super cut flower and make a great spectacle when, alas, so much of our golden colour is fading.

September is also very much spring bulb planting month, with the exception of tulips, which are best left until October. By the way, make sure that prepared hyacinth bulbs for Christmas flowering are potted by the 15th.

As the summer displays fade, clear out your hanging baskets and containers and replace the top half with fresh compost. For winter/early spring displays, plant with dwarf bulbs, winter pansies, violas, dwarf iris, crocus, heathers and ivies to lighten up the dark and dreary months to come.

As crops finish, start your winter digging as early as possible. Little and often eases the effort and, if it's chilly, always dig facing the wind...your back will thank you for this!

As always, it's all about planning.

This is the time of year when in village halls and community centres right across the country, keen gardeners are vying with each other to decide whose exhibits are the best. Time to take a look at your own garden...

Plants that allow you to put on your own 'summer show' whilst at the same time helping you to maximise available space, or to screen unsightly garden features, surely deserve a closer look.

These plants are, of course, climbers. The selection described here all offer exciting yellow flowers right through summer into autumn. Clematis is a garden favourite and Bill Mackenzie is an absolute star, producing open, bell-shaped, nodding flowers. Golden Tiara is a more compact variety, with slightly smaller flowers and reaching 8/9ft - great in limited space.

Clematis is a garden favourite and Bill Mackenzie is an absolute star

Clematis Tangutica produces yellow, bell-shaped flowers, often referred to as the orange peel clematis, due to its thick yellow sepals. Each variety requires strong support, ideally by trellis. Planting in fertile, humus-rich soil with sun to partial shade is ideal.

Climbing roses can help to bring garden features like pergolas and arbours to life. Great performers to consider are Rose Casino, which produces fragrant yellow flowers, and Rosa Golden Showers, which has glossy, dark green leaves and numerous, fragrant, clear yellow flowers in clusters.

Rose Laura Ford is a shorter growing variety with yellow, lightly scented flowers. All are fully hardy and thrive in full sun and a humus rich soil. Prune late autumn to early spring.

No coverage of climbers would be complete without a mention of Lonicera (honeysuckle). Three great honeysuckles that offer yellow flowers at this time of year are Lonicera Xamericana, L. Periclemenum Graham Thomas and L. Tragophylla.

Each is fully hardy and vigorous. L. Periclemenum particularly benefits from being pruned back to young, strong growth after flowering. The others need only to be kept in shape and pruned to fit the space available.

Most garden soils are suitable and full sun poses no problem. Everyone has space for more climbers and for any homeowner with an ugly wall, fence or tank to mask, they are a great help. Plant any of these and enjoy a glorious splash of yellow each year.

GARDEN TIPS

- Autumn clean-up time. Wash and disinfect all seed trays, pots, garden canes, etc, before storing away for the winter.
- Rough dig all vacant patches of your veg plot as they become empty. Leave in ridges for the winter weather to penetrate.

The clematis: Probably the easiest and most versatile of all our climbers

I'M GLAD ALL OVER TO BE OUT OF STEP

Over the last couple of weeks I've been able to take advantage of the good weather and all the joys a garden can give. However, snob value and keeping up with the Jones's certainly enters the equation in all branches, according to many members of the gardening media.

Yes, it's a funny old world, for two totally different plant species are very much in evidence and performing nobly in my patch, yet neither is rated highly by the purists.

I'm delighted to report that common sense has prevailed

The first is the African marigold, which I've planted in profusion this year in my garden, and which has flowered its socks off since the end of June.

Being F1 hybrids, these marigolds are uniform in height and such a sparkling rich orange colour with masses of blooms up to four inches in diameter. Perhaps not for the purist but massed with salvias and dwarf Abutilon Bella, they certainly work for me.

The second plant family not in vogue, despite the publicity by Dame Edna, is the gladioli. Thanks to its vast colour range and the many types that are available, from giant towering five feet showstoppers to exquisite tiny primulinas, there really is a 'glad' for everyone.

Grown from dormant corms, they are easy and reliable and, apart from thrips, pest-free. As a bonus, they are not expensive, especially when one considers the incredible flower power they represent. I cannot think of a colour/bi-colour not covered by them, so include them in your plans for next year. You'll be glad you did.

Over many years of extolling the merits of gardening, one of my delights has been delving into folklore and tried and tested tips and remedies that have stood the test of time.

The recent EC ruling on so many products has curtailed the use of so many of these, frankly, without justification in so many cases. Therefore, I'm delighted to report that common sense has prevailed, at least for one product, namely, bicarbonate of soda.

This household chemical has been used for centuries as a fungicide, in particular, against powdery mildew. All head gardeners of the past used this extensively, in particular on grape vines, and it has now been re-approved with a recommended dose of 3oz per gallon of water.

Yes, it's a funny old world!

GARDEN TIPS

- Green flowers are always sought-after. Why not try gladioli? Varieties include Green Woodpecker, with green and red throat or Green Star, which is ruffled and lime green.

- Keep greenhouse paths damp in hot weather to deter red spider mite.

African marigolds, which I've planted in profusion this year in my garden

Orange order: Flowerbed showing the vigour and colour of African Marigolds (note the uniform height due to it being an F1 hybrid type)

LOOK AFTER THE GREEN, GREEN GRASS OF HOME

Yes, as the Sheffield saying goes, it's all go in the big works! September is a vital time for action on our lawns, that hard working, slow-to-complain vital part of so many gardens.

After the long summer with high temperatures and dry spells, our lawns need TLC to both face the winter and give a flying start next spring.

Spiking and hollow tining are most beneficial, followed by an application of an autumn/winter-type lawn dressing. May I stress, you'll need an autumn/winter formulation, not a high nitrogen spring/summer type? Apply your dressing evenly and, for a large lawn, a wheeled applicator is a great investment.

After the long summer with high temperatures and dry spells, our lawns need TLC to both face the winter and give a flying start next spring.

Two autumn lawn pests that need prompt attack around this time are chafer grubs (a white crescent-shaped grub) and leather jackets (dark brown), the larvae of the crane fly (daddy long legs to you and me). Both feed on grass roots, turning the grass yellow/brown and creating bare patches.

Modern science has given us a natural killer for each in the form of living nematodes – one for each pest. They do work. I've just treated my lawns with both following success last year. Natural predators for so many pests are now widely available, and many of the larger retailers now have installed fridges to offer fresh supplies direct.

Autumn jobs: Lawn treatment makes grass grow healthily

Finally, to new householders, now is the time to lay a new lawn. Aim to have this completed by the end of October at the latest. Turf or seed, you cry? Well, the choice must be yours. However, the ground preparation is the most essential item so do it well and, if buying turf, do check and ask around. You get what you pay for and I regret to say I do hear some appalling stories.

LAWN TIPS

- When applying lawn dressings, 4x3ft canes should be used to mark out each square yard. Weigh out the correct amount of dressing into a plastic beaker and mark with a pen. It saves repeated weighing.

- Keep mowing your lawns but set the blades higher for autumn – a minimum of one inch high.

Whilst everything is still fresh in my memory, let me put together a brief resume of my own findings and results this year. As a garden broadcaster and journalist, I attempt to grow a wide range of plants, including my own tried and tested favourites and many new varieties that are heavily promoted. This is to form my own opinion and is a responsibility that one should not take lightly for the public do deserve to be impartially informed. So, here goes.

After the hot, dry summer, gazanias have not given the same superb display this year, but this was to be expected. Busy Lizzies have been, and still are, outstanding. What a treat they are with their self-cleaning ability (no dead heading required).

One of the stars of my containers has been Abutilon Bella; do give it earnest consideration for next season. Readers may remember I made it my bloom of the year four years ago on its introduction and this summer it has been outstanding.

I raised mine from seed, although it is also available as plugs, and have used it quite extensively. It's compact, grows to a height of approximately 12 inches and has the most attractive bells in delicate pastel shades, supported by fine foliage and again, still looks a picture. Needs a sheltered spot.

Dichondra Silver Falls - strongly featured by yours truly, has again excelled in both hanging baskets and as a border plant to cascade down taller containers. A new, green version has been bred but, frankly, the original silver is by far the superior one.

Lavatera Novella has been my star newcomer; praise indeed for I'm not usually a lavatera fan. However, its colour, compactness and sheer flower power have been great, with Dianthus Corona a very close second. This gave uniform height and a long flowering season.

My dwarf sunflowers have not covered themselves in glory this season, being very short-lived. These I reserve judgment on, for the season has not been conducive to sun lovers.

However, saving the best till last, may I remind readers of Impatiens Fiesta. This has been around for some years but still remains by far the number one double Busy Lizzy. Supreme tiny rosebud-like flowers, a good range of colours available and it literally flowers its head off! Yes, it may appear rather pricey, but accept no alternative. Frankly, I think it's a snip at the price.

GARDEN TIPS

When clearing away peas/beans/sweet peas, cut the old stems at ground level. Compost the top growth but dig in the roots. Remember, as legumes, the roots contain a store of nitrogen, so valuable for next year's crops.

Pot up prepared hyacinths now to have them in bloom for Christmas.

Top marks: Abutilon Bella

JOBS FOR OCTOBER

LAWNS: Pick a dry spell to scarify, hollow tine then apply an autumn/winter lawn fertiliser. Will ensure a great lawn next year.

GREENHOUSE: Pot up all types of spring bulbs. Ventilate well on all mild days. Bring into greenhouse all semi-tender plants like Datura, Osteospurmums, Pelargoniums, etc. Make sure all seed and plug plants are on order.

FLOWER BEDS/BORDERS: Continue to plant spring bulbs. Plant wallflowers, inter-spaced with tall tulips to make a wonderful May display.

VEGETABLE PATCH: Firm in sprouts/broccoli. Dig all vacant parts, lime the area designated for brassicas/legumes. Take out runner bean and sweet pea trenches then dust with lime.

OCTOBER

Over the last decade, this has been a golden, mellow month. Rudbeckias, Michaelmas daisies and, until the first frosts, dahlias, still give lots of colour. You may see a second flush of delphiniums and lupins, or a third or even fourth flush of rose. Magnolias and wisterias can often make a spirited attempt to bloom again. Enjoy them all.

Bulb planting in gardens and pots should be a major activity this month. Bulbs are virtually idiot-proof, as the embryo flower is formed in the bulb. All you have to do is plant them, but you can do some things to improve their performance. On garden beds, work in either a balanced fertiliser or bone meal at 2oz per square yard, and sulphate or potash at 1oz per square yard.

The key to planting bulbs is to plant them at the correct depth. Take a tip from the commercial growers who farm daffs like potatoes: plant deep at between four to six inches in light soil.

Do consider as wide a range of bulbs as possible, both for your gardens and for your pots, to give colour and cheer through the darkest winter days. Don't forget your hanging baskets either... planted with dwarf bulbs they will light up your porch in February and March.

Leaf mould is a superb soil conditioner, moisture-retaining agent and potting compost ingredient, and it's so easy to make. Try to collect leaves as soon as they fall. All types are valuable, but oak and beech are the 'pick of the crop', and they will be wasted in your compost bin. Try my method of using black polythene bin liner-type bags to make rich, friable leaf mould. Simply stuff the fresh leaves into the bags and, when full, add a dusting of compost activator. Water the leaves if they are dry, then punch a few holes into the bag for drainage. Then simply tie up the top of the bags and store in a sheltered spot. It takes 18 months to process, but the end product is fantastic – and best of all, it's free!

Lastly, why not take time out from the garden while the evenings are dark to brush up on your garden diary and gardening notes? Make notes for next year's campaign while the present year's successes and failures are still fresh in your mind. Remember – your garden is a blank canvas on which to create your very own masterpiece!

COVER UP TIME FOR MANY GARDEN TREASURES

The darker evenings, a chill in the air and strengthening winds are all signs that autumn and winter are upon us. Yes, it's cover up time for many of our garden treasures to ensure they'll be with us next year.

Greenhouses, coldframes, cloches and horticultural fleece all have a part to play in our quest for plant survival over the coming months. Start by checking your greenhouse or coldframe for broken/cracked glass and replace where needed. Greenhouse heaters need both cleaning and checking - pay particular attention to the thermostat if one is fitted. Plastic bubble sheeting is great for lining our greenhouses, but take care not to cover louvers and ventilators, for fresh air is still vital.

I make full use of plastic cloches of all types, the bell shape are a great favourite of mine due to the wide range of sizes, clarity and efficiency. These I use on such diverse items as mint, winter lettuce, osteospurmums, tender fuschias and the not so humble rhubarb. Yes, I know, an old bottomless bucket placed over a clump does well - particularly if some old manure is heaped around - but my earliest picking is always from under a large plastic bell cloche. This I line with black plastic to exclude light.

Rhubarb is very much the 'in thing' with many notable chefs and cookery experts at the moment, probably due to its earliness, versatility and, of course, the premium price it demands in January/February when it is an early treat in the Jackson household - rhubarb crumble being a particular favourite.

Rhubarb is very much the 'in thing' with many notable chefs

Rhubarb forcing: Rhubarb just uncovered and a bell cloche used

GARDEN TIPS

It's time to take cuttings of fuschias, surfinias, geraniums, etc, for over-wintering in a greenhouse. Take small, non-flowering tip cuttings.

After the recent storms collect all apple 'windfalls' - if sound, use immediately as they will not store well. Surplus can be pureed.

MAKE YOUR MIND UP TIME

A regular problem facing gardeners around this time of year is more pronounced than ever this season. I refer to the planting of spring bulbs not only in our beds and borders, but also in our containers and hanging baskets.

We are all loath to foreclose on our summer displays; after all, they've done us really proud this season and are still performing well for many, but it is definitely time for planting bulbs - daffodils, in particular. Whilst they can be planted later and give a great display, planting now gives a better root formation and stouter stems and foliage.

Planting tulips can be left for a week or two but do give these colourful, exotic flowers pride of place, due to the versatility and fantastic range. They belie their tender looks by being far tougher than they look. Yes, I accept a little shelter is paramount for the taller types but they really can stand their share of adverse weather.

In my book they come into their own and excel in containers and hanging baskets, and are best planted in bold patches of one variety, rather than mixed. I base this on the fact that each variety has its own specific flowering date.

Apart from the exotic petal forms, such as parrot, lily flowered, double and multi-headed, to name but a few, tulip foliage can give added charm. Examples of this are in the dwarf types with dark, mahogany striped leaves which make a great foil for the following flower heads.

Tulips can, and do, naturalise well. All they ask is a fairly deep rich root run.

Planting, as with all bulbs, should be approximately twice the depth of the bulb height, and don't forget to give a light dressing of bone meal to ensure a good root system.

When buying tulips - as with all bulbs - if at all possible do the thumb test. That is, press with your thumb under the bulb base to ensure solid flesh with no base rot. Tulip skins can often become detached in travelling/packing/handling. This isn't a problem, so long as the flesh is creamy white with no obvious major blemishes.

Enjoy your tulips.

In my book they come into their own and excel in containers and hanging baskets, and are best planted in bold patches of one variety

TULIP TIPS

- Try forcing in a coldframe/ greenhouse a pot or two of miniature types for mid-winter colour.

- A word of caution. Wear rubber gloves when handling dry tulip and hyacinth bulbs, as quite a few people develop a rash from them.

Daffodils and tulips: An excellent addition to any bed or border

Hether it's due to the gardening media or the cookery experts I know not, but the news from all sources that home grown produce is very much the 'in thing' gladdens my heart. Yes, all the major seedsmen agree that there is definitely a dramatic upturn in sales for both vegetable seeds and plug plants. Good on you!

The tiniest garden can produce so much in vegetable and salad crops, thanks to modern methods and varieties. In fact, with growbags, containers, etc, all that is required is outdoor standing space.

Now is the time to take action by firstly drawing up your plans and deciding on a programme for next year.

Spuds have never been more in vogue and I'm inundated with information on new varieties for the coming year. Remember, they are ideal for either pot growing or for planting in a raised bed; either way, several types are widely available.

Go for first or second early varieties where the emphasis is on taste. The secret is to grow them in rich compost and when planting your pre-chitted seed potatoes, only just cover them. As the foliage (haulm) grows, top-up slowly and regularly and give lots of weak liquid feed. Seed potatoes are available from November/December so get cracking with your order.

Outdoor tomatoes are a great crop; the essential here is picking the correct growing spot. A sheltered, warm, south or southwest facing bed or patio is ideal. Don't start too early; planting in mid-June of stocky, well-hardened plants is early enough and don't forget Tumbler and Tumbling Tom Red are both great varieties for hanging baskets or containers.

Growbags are so very versatile and for the not-so-nimble, place them on a low trestle support - 3ft is an ideal height. A mixed salad crop will provide great variety, i.e. lettuce, radish, spring onion, stumpy carrots, etc.

For the sweet-toothed, do consider strawberries. Set twelve plants to a full sized growbag or in a hanging basket, but when

The ultimate: A dazzling, colourful display of veg and salad crops at Chelsea. Inset: "Veg King" Medwyn Williams, with his award-winning vegetables at the Chelsea Flower Show

blossom is set, do cover with a net to keep our feathered friends away from the ripening fruit.

Yes, even for non-garden owners, colour, taste and variety can be yours. The new catalogues are full of both new and tried and tested mini fruit and veg, so take up the challenge...it's good for you!

GARDEN TIPS

- After clearing beds and borders, take a pH test of your soil. Remember, if needed, now is the time to apply lime.

- Order bare rooted roses, fruit trees and canes for November delivery and planting. Prepare the site now, and for raspberries, have the supporting stakes inserted at each end of the rows.

A BOUNTIFUL TIME FOR ALL GARDENERS AS LEAVES FALL

Yes, it's bonanza time - 'freebie' time - as our trees, woods and coppices are about to disgorge a bountiful free harvest. As Jackson often remarks - "fill your boots!"

I refer of course to falling leaves and that magic bounty they produce: leaf mould. As a youngster I well remember the many trips I took to the Rivelin/Bradfield wooded areas in October and November for this bonus, which is guaranteed each year.

Leaves, which of course are the lungs of a plant, are truly remarkable for, having completed their first life cycle, have a second major role to play for us if we only seek them out and collect. It is difficult to under-estimate the true value of leaf mould for it is so complex yet so valuable and child's play to produce.

Obviously totally organic, they are so rich a source of humus, that living entity of our soil and the basis of fertility. Probably the finest soil conditioner known to man yet it's free for the asking!

LEAF MOULD TIPS

- Add a handful of bonemeal to a bucketful of leaf mould and use under trees/shrubs when planting new stock - gets them off to a flying start.

- As above but use fish, blood and bone. Use a mulch in existing climbers, rose beds, fruit canes. Apply three inches deep in spring.

Some experts suggest that fallen leaves be added to your compost heap, but unless you only have a very limited source, I disagree. In my book they are too valuable and deserve a pride of place all of their own.

Basically all fresh fallen leaves are suitable, with beech and oak being the best. The accent should be on fresh, but if you have permitted access to woodlands, scraping away the surface layer around tall trees reveals layers of dark, rich and crumbly, years old, ready-made leaf mould - pure magic.

Collecting is so simple; I still find the black bin liner/old compost bags ideal. Just rake them up and stuff your bags to bursting. It is so light and sweet smelling, and your garden will give thanks by much better results.

Storing, even in a small garden, need not be a problem. Fill your bags, water if dry, add an activator (there is a special formulation for leaves), tie up the bags, and puncture a few holes to admit air - job's done.

Place in any 'out of the way' spot outdoors, such as the back of a garden, the shed or garage. The longer you leave them the better.

Should you have the space available, a square or rectangular pen made with four posts and chicken wire makes a superb leaf-mould factory. When full, cover with an old carpet to retain moisture and let nature do its work.

So do join me on leaf collecting and composting, it's a rewarding experience.

Future use: Nature's own humus factory! A view of woodland before leaf fall

JOBS FOR NOVEMBER

ROSES: 'Step' prune climbers for a good spread of bloom. Cut back alternate branches hard each year.

BUSH ROSES: Cut tall bushes back half way to reduce wind-rock, but wait until March for main pruning.

FRUIT TREES/BUSHES: A great month to plant new stock - plant firmly and stake on a well-prepared site.

VEGETABLE PATCH: Finish winter digging, carry out a pH test and lime where needed.

GREENHOUSE: Wash glass, etc. If empty, burn a sulphur candle to sterilise the greenhouse. At the end of the month bring advanced pots of spring bulbs into a warm greenhouse to have blooms at Christmas.

TIDY UP: Take out sweet pea/runner bean trenches. Cover compost with old carpets. Wash pots, seed trays, garden canes. Check fences - winter is coming!

NOVEMBER

November...the month when late chrysanthemums hold centre stage.

A senior citizen listener phoned my phone-in last November complaining that she could not find these large blooms, which had been commonplace in her youth. My answer was that, regrettably, they are no longer commercially viable so have virtually disappeared. But, worry not, you can still grow your own. All that's needed is time, patience, a little know-how, a small patch of open garden and a small greenhouse.

Sounds a lot, but the end result is sheer joy. Visit chrysant shows and talk to the exhibitors; you'll be impressed with their enthusiasm and their desire to help and give advice.

On to practical matters...

Soil testing is a "must" for all keen gardeners. Remember, like our plants, our soil is constantly changing. The simple, inexpensive DIY tests that are widely available are surprisingly accurate, but specialist laboratories can be located if need be.

November is also the time for liming your soil. Do remember that lime and manure are not compatible so use lime (if needed) in autumn and delay applying manure until spring, or vice versa depending on your garden's soil type.

This is also the month to carry out repairs and maintenance of all your tools, equipment, fixtures and fittings.

COTINUS FOR COLOUR

Colour in the garden creates mood and is a key building block in the design process. Generally we look to flowers for the exciting reds, relaxing blues and warm yellows and oranges. Shades of green tend to be the staple for the foliage of shrubs, hedging and trees that provide structure for all, or part, of the year. However, there are some really exciting shrubs and small trees that offer different colours of foliage, which can really transform your garden into something out of the ordinary.

For a sense of affluence, a calming feel and a fulsome, well-rounded look, species and varieties of cotinus have lots to offer. Also known as Smoke Bush because of the smoke-like appearance of its delicate flower clusters, many varieties produce purple foliage that can transform the look of a border.

For a sense of affluence, a calming feel and a well-rounded look, cotinus has lots to offer

Cotinus also has the presence to be effective on its own as a specimen plant in the garden. By using plants with different coloured leaves, you can provide attractive contrast with the greens of shrubs, trees and lawns and give flowering plants an interesting background. Cotinus Coggygria offers beautiful varieties that will bring the benefits of purple foliage to the garden. Royal Purple produces dark red/purple leaves that turn scarlet in autumn; a bushy tree or shrub that, at maturity, reaches a height and spread of 20-feet or more. Grace is slightly bigger with oval, purple leaves that turn a brilliant red in late autumn.

All of these will work equally well in a shrub border or as specimen plants. Where space is limited in small gardens, do remember they can be kept in check by judicious pruning.

This treatment has an added bonus with cotinus, which responds to pruning by putting on extra large leaves. If there is space to allow them to reach full size, the only maintenance needed is a tidy up in late winter/early spring.

Cotinus is fully hardy and will thrive in most garden soils provided they are moderately fertile, and well-drained but moist. The purple-leaved varieties mentioned produce their best colour effects in full sun.

Working with colour can achieve great results, whatever the size of your garden. Make the glorious greens even more enjoyable by providing a visual contrast and, for extra effect, use the purple of cotinus as a colourful backdrop to flowering plants.

Yes, smoking may be bad for you but, rest assured, a well-grown smoke bush should fill you with a great sense of well-being.

GARDEN TIPS

- Do clear leaves from paths and driveways - they really can prove a slippery menace. Also clear your greenhouse and shed gutters of the same.

- Store hosepipes under cover to avoid frost damage and either cover outside water taps or turn off the supply completely - winter is just around the corner.

Cotinus: A splendid specimen plant to provide a stunning colour foliage

Whilst our plant raisers beaver away in their efforts to produce bigger and better varieties in all segments of our beloved hobby, the growing media boffins are also doing their bit.

Yes, it's the "new goodies" in the plant world that grab the headlines, but without the current feeds, growing techniques and equipment, their full potential could not be reached.

The general desire to reduce the use of peat continues unabated

The general desire to reduce the use of peat continues unabated, but a completely satisfactory replacement is not yet with us, although progress continues. The mystique that shrouds composts in general is, for many, a minefield. Let me attempt to simplify this:

SOIL-BASED COMPOSTS

John Innes is the flag bearer and comes in four grades, namely, Seed, No.1, No. 2 and No. 3. Seed is a very low nutrient level, ideal for seed sowing and rooting soft wood cuttings, like chrysanthemums, fuschias, dahlias, geraniums, etc. Numbers 1, 2 and 3 are best described as low, medium and high in nutrients respectively. So, No. 1 is for rooted cuttings/seedlings in, say, a 3" to 4" pot; No. 2 is for bigger young plants in a 5" or 6" pot; and No. 3 is best for larger plants in 8" diameter pots and upwards.

When buying John Innes compost, always look for brands bearing the "John Innes Compost Makers' Association" label to ensure uniformity.

PEAT & PEAT-FREE COMPOSTS

These come in just two major types. Firstly "universal" or "multi-purpose" (the definition varies) and "potting". Note: there are two choices as opposed to four in soil-based composts.

The first type contains a medium amount of fertiliser, attempting to be suitable for both seed-raising and potting on - something of a compromise being all things to all plants. This is by far the biggest seller, ideal for the gardener who only dabbles in a small way, but can give variable results.

The other major type is "potting", higher in nutrients so for bigger, more advanced plants.

However many of our leading compost producers have progressed further with special mixes in ericaceous (for lime-hating plants), hanging baskets, containers, vegetables, tomatoes, etc. All are designed to give better results in a chosen field.

I trust I've shed some light on a complex yet vital matter, but remember; personal results are what really count.

COMPOST TIPS

- Liquid feeding is always essential but for long term subjects add slow release fertiliser and water retaining granules to make life easier.

- Add extra grit to composts for alpines etc to improve drainage.

"Bedders": Note root formation and good leaf colour - due to quality compost, plus TLC!

BE COOL AND GO FOR HIGHLY PRIZED GREEN FLOWERS

The coolness of green is both soothing and restful, and a favourite colour amongst flower arrangers and floral art enthusiasts. Foliage is available in every shade of green, including striped and bi-coloured, and there are a few choice flowers in green that are highly prized.

A great favourite that has stood the test of time is Molucella - Bells of Ireland. This has been around for ever, it seems, but still worthy of a place in every garden for its stately column of pale green bells. Actually a native of Syria, grow it as a HHA and use either fresh or dried.

Nicotiana is another very popular family of HH annuals that comes in many colours with at least two recommended green varieties, namely, from the Domino Series, Lime Green, which grows approximately twelve inches high, and Green Goddess; taller at approximately twenty inches and probably the greenest of all. Both these have upward facing flowers so give a bold display, and are equally suitable as cut flowers.

Hostas are everyone's favourite, including slugs and snails, with their stately spear-shaped foliage with many bi-colours that are both cool and aristocratic - a true blue-blooded plant with flowers as a bonus. This year I've probably had my best show ever with virtually no slug damage. This, I feel, is due to the sheer size of my mature plants. Container growing hostas is one way to deter slugs, and why not consider them for hanging baskets? After all, as yet, slugs don't fly!

My green newcomer, however, is one I unearthed on my visit to Ball Colgrave's press day in 2004, namely Zinnia Lime Green Ball. This is a classic ball-shape; dwarf but still tall enough to cut for display.

I'm sure this new variety will prove a winner, not only for flower arrangers, but all who seek the cooling effect of lime green. It will look great when grown with contrasting purple foliage or blooms.

Zinnias are a particular favourite of mine, revelling in hot summer weather and producing long lasting flowers of precise form. Do remember, however, they do best grown in cell trays, one seed per cell, as they object strongly to root disturbance.

So, in the earnest wish for a long, hot summer, let's go green! Here's hoping.

Zinnias are a particular favourite of mine, revelling in hot weather

GARDEN TIPS

- After the recent frosty nights, cover a clump of rhubarb with either an old bucket or large cloche to produce juicy stalks for January. Also mulch with old manure/compost.

- Wrap outdoor containers with bubble wrap to help keep contents frost-free.

Zinnia: Lime Green Ball

The British horticultural industry has, sadly, been in steady decline over the last few years, but who is to blame?

Is it cheap imports from the 'mega plant factories' in Holland, the increasing new threat of expanding production from the Iberian Peninsular who enjoy much higher temperatures and have lower labour costs, or supermarket/DIY chains selling 'bland plants', i.e. bedders, mass produced shrubs, roses and climbers by the million? Whatever the reason, the small family-run nursery is suffering badly.

I refer to the true plantsmen and women who put quality plants, free advice and expertise before profit.

I'm old enough to remember, before gardening centres were a gleam in the bank manager's eye, when plants were sold by the same person that raised them from a seed or cutting, nurtured them with TLC, and then sold them by the score wrapped in newspaper and handed over with free advice on how to look after them.

Yes, pure nostalgia but treasured memories best described by that gardening guru, Beth Chatto, as 'handmade plants'.

Of course price is important, but I do suggest when buying plants to compare like with like. We can all pick up a bag of desiccated bulbs or a climber of dubious vigour in a glossy poly bag with our groceries, but do our gardens not deserve better?

Without our specialist family nurseries, our gardens could become bland, homogenised areas akin to flat pack stereotyped furniture lacking depth and structure.

It is often said that a garden reflects the owner and is a personal thing. This I subscribe to, and also to the belief that a garden should be continually evolving.

With this in mind I earnestly suggest we take a close look at our buying policy and support the true British nurserymen who, in my view, have

Labour of love: A superb, prize-winning display from a local nursery

no equal. The saying 'use it or lose it' springs to mind and I feel fortunate to have lived in the era of 'proper' growers, to whom plants were a way of life.

Visiting shows, both local and national, is a real education for the sheer love of plants, enthusiasm and comradeship that is evident with the true nurseryman and shines like a beacon. Do support them, for sadly, I fear, they are a dying breed and you surely can't put a price on expertise and know-how.

GARDEN TIPS

- After your final cut – hopefully – of your lawn, do have your mower serviced and cleaned ready for next season.

- Helleborus Niger (Christmas Rose) – put up a young plant and place in a cold greenhouse to make a great Christmas houseplant or place a clear plastic cloche over a large outdoor specimen to give cut blooms for Christmas.

JOBS FOR DECEMBER

LAWN: Compost fallen leaves but keep off the lawn when it is wet or frosty.

FLOWER BEDS: Keep your containers dry and raise with pot feet or bricks to prevent from freezing.

VEGETABLE PATCH: Tidy up loose ends and continue forcing and planting salad crops.

FRUIT: Prune secondary growth on apples and pears.

GREENHOUSE: This is an ideal time to take cutting of carnations (Diananthus).

DECEMBER

A month to reflect on past seasons...

Pot up and bring into a cool room or heated greenhouse any Christmas roses (Helleborus Niger) that show early buds. They make excellent centrepieces at the Christmas dinner table and are always a great talking point.

Sprigs of winter jasmine (Jasminum Nudiflorum) that are showing their first tiny yellow buds should be cut and placed in deep water around the 18th December to (hopefully) open and give beauty and perfume, which is divine, on Christmas Day.

May I suggest you consider joining one or more of the specialist gardening societies that abound? The choice of society is quite frankly enormous, each with local and regional members, meetings, shows, newsletters, and so on.

The number one, of course, the Royal Horticultural Society, is a national treasure and rightly so. But do look around to see what else is available. The fees are truly peppercorn as they are all non-profit making organisations staffed by true enthusiasts (or, dare I say it, near fanatics!) who give up their time and expertise so willingly.

Organic gardeners should consider joining "Grow Organic", formerly known for many years as the "Henry Doubleday Research Association" with the head office and trial grounds at Ryton near Coventry.

I have been an active member of many societies, both local and national, and derived so much from them. Allotment growing is very much on the upturn, and long may it continue for this is where I started. Their relevant association is the "National Society of Allotment and Leisure Gardeners", with headquarters based in Corby, Northants. A very 'go-ahead' society with lots to offer.

Finally, settle down with a glass of falling down water and congratulate yourself on a successful year of gardening.

Merry Christmas!

At this time of year, the buzzword for so many is spring bulbs – such great, unassuming performers. Yes, I agree, it is early but let us look at a different range of bulbous spring and summer charmers, ornamental alliums – onions to you and me.

My overwhelming memory of the first BBC Gardeners' World Exhibition a few years ago was the tremendous interest created by a massed display by RV Rogers & Sons, the long-established North Yorkshire nursery. They certainly created a furore with hundreds of alliums in full bloom.

Whilst not all have spherical flower heads, the majority do and, coupled with their stately stems, they make a great presence in our borders. Colours range widely and the fleshy, strap-like foliage gives a solid, no-nonsense frame. Very much pest and disease-free, they naturalise well.

Planting should be in batches or clumps – three or five is ideal – and make sure you allow space to develop. On heavy soil, a handful of grit sand in each planting hole assists drainage and bone meal is a real help in their first year.

Bulbs can be left for several years, only lift and divide, as with all bulbs, when they appear congested. Planting can be carried out in either late autumn or spring and the flowering period runs from April to August, depending on variety.

Some of my favourites – all spherical – include Allium Giganteum which, as the name suggests, makes its presence felt by being a stately four feet high with stunning five inch diameter pink flower heads.

Allium Schubertii has a sparkler-like head that really erupts in colour and is just over one foot high. Allium Azureum is electric blue and as a companion or contrast, try Allium Karatavense, a white dwarf variety ten inches high and ideal on a rockery. Allium Christophii is star shaped, bright pink and two feet high. The choice is really wide and, as a bonus, they

alliums are a flower lover's delight

Floral fireworks: Ornamental onions are a wonderful addition to the garden

make long-lasting cut flowers and can be dried for floral art and winter displays.

From my recommendations you will note there are some choice dwarf varieties, although the tall, stately types really have a commanding grace. So remember, apart from all the edible family members, alliums are also a flower lover's delight.

Enjoy your onions many ways.

ORNAMENTAL ONION TIPS

- Always plant at least four inches deep; a mulch of straw/ compost in winter protects them from hard frosts.

- As with all bulbs, they are not happy out of the ground so plant promptly on receipt.

The culmination of the cold weather and the vast increase in the available supply of pot plants has prompted me to launch a new society - the NSPCCPP - please give it your fullest support.

What do the letters refer to, you ask? Namely, the National Society for the Prevention of Cruelty to Christmas Pot Plants. Yes, I'm thinking of the countless plants standing on garage forecourts, market stalls and outside shops. Poor little perishers! You buy them with hard-earned cash but, so often, they are doomed to failure as they have received a fatal chill.

It is sad to think that after they have been so carefully raised over many months, they fail at this final stage. Do buy from a reliable source, select with care, ensure the plants are well wrapped for their journey home, and keep inside the car, not the icy boot for the homeward journey.

Amongst the many Christmas pot plants, may I select the poinsettia, a member of the Euphorbia family. The traditional scarlet bracts so exude the Christmas spirit, but do remember our boffins have now given us other shades and colours, including pink, white, cream and marbled, to extend the range.

When buying, look for a strong, firm, youthful appearance and pay special attention to the tiny yellow flowers at the very top. These should be closed and fresh, not open or faded.

They are grown by specialist nurseries who give them, by the use of black-out blinds in the greenhouses, long night/short day treatment to induce the coloured bracts for Christmas. Treating them with a dwarf retarding chemical and high potash liquid feed keeps them dwarf and bushy.

In the Azores and Madeira, their natural habitat, they make colourful, towering hedges of up to eight feet high in May and June. To give off their best, they require good light, a medium temperature - around 55-60°F is ample - and a humid atmosphere, so mist frequently. Don't over-water and allow the leaves to nearly drop before watering thoroughly.

Poinsettia: There are many shades to give Christmas cheer

Perhaps the most regular question I receive about the poinsettia, is "how do I get it to bloom again next Christmas?" So here goes:

POINSETTIA TIPS

- As with all pot plants, always use water at room temperature.

- Always best to water from below - stand in a shallow dish of water, then allow to drain away excess.

1. In May, cut back hard down to three to four inches and re-pot.

2. Stand outside in full sun from June until first week in October.

3. Bring back under cover and every evening cover with black plastic bag/cardboard box from 6pm till 8am the following day.

4. Give regular doses of weak, high potash fertiliser.

5. By December, it should be back in full colour. Best of luck!

PLANT A TREE AND PUT DOWN SOME ROOTS FOR POSTERITY

Apart from commercial growers who, of course, grow for profit, we amateurs grow either for eating, exhibiting, or just for the sheer feeling of enjoyment and the warm glow of achievement.

May I suggest a further reason? Namely, for the future generations and posterity: yes, plant a tree for many generations to come.

It is a sobering, nay frightening, statistic that the UK has the lowest wooded areas in the whole of mainland Europe. May I urge you all to try and redress the balance?

As folklore tells us, from the tiny acorn the mighty oak tree grew

Our climate lends itself to many species of trees, both evergreen and deciduous, and I promise, you will get real satisfaction growing a tree from scratch. Whilst it is true to say that you are growing for the next generation or two, I'm sure you'll agree with me it is more than worthwhile.

As folklore tells us, from the tiny acorn the mighty oak tree grew, and they make an ideal starting point. Whilst there are hundreds of species of oak, they all need the same cultivation.

Use fresh acorns; discard the cups and place in a dish of water. Discard any that float – only plant the ones that sink. Use the same method with both horse and sweet chestnut.

Ash, sycamore and maples produce keys, or two winged seedlings. Collect fresh and, when they turn brown, cut off the wings and sow.

All the above can be sown in pots or seed trays using John Innes seed compost with added grit. A coldframe is ideal but be prepared for slow and often erratic germination.

The important point is to grow your seedlings steadily, potting on as they develop. Guard against rabbits and squirrels in their formative years and allocate a proper site for their final home.

Local authorities, the National Trust and the Tree Council are always pleased to help, so why not take up the challenge? Always bear in mind when planting locally gathered seed, if only twenty per cent germinate, you should take that as a success, not a failure.

Many of our national seed merchants now list fresh, graded seed of many popular trees. Do soak these overnight in tepid water to re-hydrate them before sowing.

TREE SOWING TIPS

- Use clay pots for growing your seedlings – the Long Tom type being most suitable.

- Use a short cane to support seedlings in their first year or so – it does aid growth surprisingly well.

Green canopy: The sheer majesty of an English wooded valley

SOME SEASONAL THOUGHTS AS DAYS GROW SHORTEST

At this time of year, when we have the shortest days and the whole heartbeat of our garden is at its lowest ebb, it is surely the time to reflect and perhaps ponder. Yes, the year has flown by and, no doubt for you, like myself, some things worked out better than others.

However, as you know, a garden is never finished. Gardeners are never satisfied, but surely to strive for perfection isn't a bad thing. Suffice to say, we'll all tackle the New Year a little older, hopefully a little wiser and just as keen.

Walking round my patch this week, I was delighted and my spirits lifted to find winter jasmine (jasmin nudiflorum) further advanced than usual. Do include this in your garden; the graceful yellow flowers and subtle fragrance are supreme for your Christmas table. Cut when just showing colour and place in a warmish room to develop.

However, let's forget humans for the moment and spare a thought for our feathered friends. I've just received a great treasury of a free catalogue from CJ Wildbird Foods which really goes to town on all aspects of native birds - and wild mammals - in Great Britain. This is a specialist catalogue offering a great mail order service and a wealth of products, foods, recipes, ideas and bird identification pictures; you name it, they cover it.

I promise, the Jackson household does its little bit in helping the local bird population. May I suggest you place out dishes of fresh water, as this can be more important than food on some days?

I trust you have completed your winter digging. Remember, now is the ideal time to check your soil for both pH and nutrient levels. Apart from the above, take time out to relax; my ideal is a glass of falling down water, a supply of next year's seed/plant catalogues and a fairy godmother to produce a signed blank cheque!

A sincere Merry Christmas and Happy New Year to all, I've really enjoyed my year with you.

We'll all tackle the New Year a little older, hopefully a little wiser and just as keen.

GARDEN TIPS

- Should you have Christmas gift vouchers to spend, may I suggest max/min thermometers and soil or pH testing kits - all so useful.

- For the gardener who has everything, how about a load of well rotted horse manure?